629.4   Lindaman, E.B.
Lin   Space: a new direction
          for mankind.

SPACE:

●

A NEW DIRECTION FOR MANKIND

SPACE:

●

A New Direction for Mankind

EDWARD B. LINDAMAN

1817

HARPER & ROW, PUBLISHERS
NEW YORK, EVANSTON, AND LONDON

First Edition

LIBRARY OF CONGRESS CATALOG CARD NUMBER: 78-85043

1308

CONTENTS

●   Contents

●   Contents

Looking for the star
Religion in flux
Deciphering God's blueprints
What place is left for God?
Can we tune in each other?
A vision shapes us

● Contents

PREFACE

This book is an attempt to place in perspective the *total* meaning of man's exploration of Space—for it may well be an entirely new direction for man.

The filters are being removed from between us and almost everything that happens. Man's monologue with himself is over. The very universe around him now "speaks" to him through the beeping satellites and spacecraft.

I do not want to wait for historians to tell me about the excitement of exploring Space. I want to—and can—experience it *now*. This is possible for the millions of human beings around the world, if we can bridge the gap between the engineers and scientists and the common man. This book will try to begin that process.

Wherever technical terms are used they are explained. The book should not be difficult to read, even for the scientific layman. Many people are turned off by talk of Space because they think it is beyond their comprehension. Nothing is further from the truth. We have only to exercise that wonderful human faculty of manipulating new ideas inside our heads, and to replace some timeworn folk knowledge with new Space Age terms that describe the most exciting adventure in man's history. I have tried to stay away from technical jargon and unrealistic fantasy.

Every historical event that has changed man's view of the world has also changed man's understanding of himself. Now we have suddenly begun looking at the world from outside the world. We can be more critical, perhaps more detached, surely more competent in seeing it as a whole.

Man has always reacted to his world through various symbols. One of the most consistent has been the symbol of flight—a bird, an eagle. It seems to symbolize our basic urge to be free from the confines of Earth. Now man has achieved the ultimate in flight. He really is free from Earth. What will his next craving be? The answer is coming clear: it is man himself. Man must now conquer himself.

This is the new framework of our thinking, the midcourse correction in our generation's voyage. Therefore our new Space Age will be filled with social changes destined to break down human barriers, new concepts of stewardship for Earth's resources, new qualities of communication and cooperation, new and more open international dealings, and new openness to one another. The present generation is the first to see this and react to it. It is a new view, from a point in Space.

I hope the book points in the direction in which we must take our newfound capabilities, for Space truly *is* a new direction for humanity, if we choose. We will choose rightly only if we know the facts.

EDWARD B. LINDAMAN

July 23, 1969
Fullerton, California

1

THE FEAT OF THE FISH

●

Our century is not only one of overproduction and great scientific discoveries. It is also a century of famines, of leprosy, of ignorance.

It is not only a world of Space vehicles, it is also the world of those who urgently need wheelbarrows, hoes and trucks. It is not only interplanetary voyages, it is villages imprisoned in jungles and deserts.

— Sekou Toure, President of Guinea

●

America's rush into Space is in some ways the most remarkable event in our history, perhaps in the world's history. Like all huge processes, it has many meanings and is hard to see whole. The thrust into Space cannot be understood by a scanning from only one viewpoint. This book will show it in many perspectives and seek to trace its consequences in our churches, our kitchens, our sickrooms, our factories, our executive suites, our schools. We will try to see how the many roads ahead are changing—or can change, or should change—because of Space.

There is no necessary order in which Space's many sides should be seen. Hence the following chapters need not be read in the order of their appearance. The reader may wish to single out the chapters concerning those aspects of Space and Earth which interest him most.

But we might begin by reminding ourselves that everything is the sum of the past. Nothing can be understood except through its history. As our human family heads out toward the stars, it is necessary to remember our own history, and even the history of our prehuman forebears.

What a mysterious ascension life has been! From slime and star dust, from one microscopic cell miraculously born and fertilized, God has brought life forth bit by bit. We have come very far uphill since the dawn men, hour after hour, patiently chipped arrowheads and knives from stone. From there we have advanced to the writing of symphonies and the weighing of nebulae. We are now ready to move up another giant step.

Perhaps our species must go on into Space, or perhaps we must suppress our inner nature. A child in its cradle cannot lie there for a lifetime. A grub is snug in its cocoon, but when the appointed time comes it must break out, flex its new butterfly wings, and flutter away. It does not know why. But something within commands it, as something commands salmon to swim up waterfalls. Is that same evolutionary need commanding our species?

Imagine you are in your living room, watching three pet goldfish in a bowl. Suddenly they propel themselves out of their safe fishbowl, up into the air, out through a slightly open window, and away. Somehow they move at a most unfishy, bulletlike speed to a far-distant city. They tarry there a little while—not in water, but on the forbidden element of the land. Then they rise again into the alien air, find their way back to your window and into your living room and safely down again into the bowl—the single refuge known to them where warmth and food and equilibrium and something breathable are to be found.

Unbelievable? Obviously. From a cosmic viewpoint, humanity's trips through Space are just as astounding, and for virtually the same reasons.

Ten years ago such trips were quite beyond mankind's powers. Five centuries of research went into the preparations. When finally the Apollo moon ship balanced itself on a pillar of fire and soared into history, it was the apex of a pyramid based on the sum total of man's scientific knowledge. That pyramid has grown prodigiously in the last decade, through the enthusiastic toil of thousands of researchers racing a deadine.

We may ask, To what purpose has it grown? Merely to pull off a brief stunt that might give the United States more leadership among less privileged nations? Merely to get a close look at a bleak place where nothing can live and nothing of value is to be found?

Space enthusiasts make various responses. One is that the moon may have more value than can be foreseen. Another is that the stockpile of new knowledge—the forced growth of which was deliberately seeded by the old device of setting a dramatic goal—has already paved the way for material progress in many directions.

Another response, from NASA and its backers in government, is that "the moon landing only makes sense if we go on from there." The enormous expenditures, the endless sweat and tears, the great tide of science, were invoked with the long-range purpose of sweeping mankind within reach of permanent steppingstones in Space. Permanent orbiting hospitals and health resorts a few hundred miles above Earth may seem desirable and attainable as we shall later see. Other specific purposes are described later—such as mastering strange new manufacturing techniques in Space, and anchoring cosmodromes as way stations for easier trips to the moon and elsewhere. Tourist flights to the moon are not inconceivable. Exotic alloys smacking of alchemy could materialize in an unlimited vacuum where weight makes no difference, and could someday confront us with such apparitions as skyscrapers five times higher than the Empire State Building, or suspension bridges twice as long as today's longest.

Our new prowess in Space has other significance to scientists. They generally agree that expanding our knowledge of nature is worthwhile in itself, even when no immediate benefits are in view. "The universe is full of magical things, patiently waiting for our wits to grow sharper," as novelist Eden Phillpotts once observed. The compulsion to learn more and more seems as innate to scientists as is the compulsion to explore unknown places among nomads; and both kinds of men have served humanity well in the long run, even if this was not their motive.

The Space scientists' way of thinking is detailed in two chapters. Man is just beginning to discover how blind and deaf he has always been. Our world, and the supposed emptiness of interstellar Space, are drenched with colors and sounds and waves that our pitiably limited eyes and ears do not perceive. Our human organs are tuned to only a few octaves in a scale that stretches out prodigiously in both directions—from the microwaves we have just discovered coming from the sun and stars, through cosmic rays of unknown origin and peculiar effect, on to waves that are literally a mile or more in length. The atmosphere around us rings like a beaten gong with sound waves no living ear can hear; and we are part of a vast rainbow we cannot see, all light and iridescent auras invisible to human eyes. We have a whole array of instruments to detect some of this.

There are photographic plates in observatories that gaze nightlong at just one black patch of sky. Where we see only nothingness, the sensitive film gathers on its surface enough photons of light to build up a picture of a star that really is out there though nobody can ever see it. No human eye could stare so patiently.

In similar superhuman servitude the new radio telescopes, which can collaborate with computers to sort out the squawks and beeps and crackles emitted billions of years ago by galaxies that may be dead long since, have lately doubled the limits of the perceptible universe. And we know now that clouds of ionized gas, ruffling their great plumes across the black voids, are on the move though our most sensitive radios and cameras cannot find them; they reflect radar waves and disturb magnetometers, and thus by long chains of reasoning we learn of their presence. Science is dumfounded by some of the enormous shapes it has lately discerned through its new peepholes into the depths of Space. Further revelations may await astronomers when they are no longer earthbound.

What of the perennial complaint against pure science and exploration made by people who put up money: What's the pay-off for all that knowledge? Isn't it sheer waste of time and funds?

Trying to imagine the world as it will be ten years hence is now harder, and more necessary, than ever before. Margaret Mead once wrote that "anyone over forty is an immigrant to the now." The present is changing so swiftly, and becoming so complex, that even those under forty may find themselves as bewildered as immigrants just off the boat. A nation of bewildered people can be a danger to itself and to the world. "Anything that raises the level of man's imagination is good," as Barbara Ward once remarked—and probably the greatest value of our leap into Space is that it ignites our imagination and gives us a heightened sense of what is possible.

Historians and sociologists and philosophers—some of them—have been saying this about the present as seen in the perspective of the past. "Dissatisfaction with the present and a longing for renewal have been generaed in the almost universal anguish of two world wars," wrote Michael Novak, a young Catholic scholar then at Stanford University, in 1967. "There are many persons in our society whose sense of mystery has atrophied. Christianity becomes relevant for these people when it draws them into reflection on who they are and how they relate to one another." Rather unexpectedly, such reflection and renewal arise from the shock of seeing mankind in Space.

Glowing deep in the hearts of great groups of men has been a yearning for one world of mankind united in brotherhood. Innumerable Space projects are inching the world closer to unity. After all, no country can track its own satellites unaided, and the complex mechanics of Space exploration make internation teamwork necessary.

The struggle for worldwide peace and the struggle for worldwide prosperity are inseparable. Strange as it may seem to nontechnical people, satellites are already doing much to promote prosperity, pull villages out of their imprisonment, point the way to more productive farms and mines and wells and factories.

But our satellites and Space ships are agents of progress on another level too. A pride of achievement has rolled around the world. The bridging of Space is an unprecedented accomplishment by the whole human race. It shows that nothing is now impossible for us when we put our minds to it. And it shows the contrast between what we have done and what is still left undone, as President Toure points out in the quotation that begins this chapter. Gray looks much darker when set against white. Seeing ourselves in Space gives us a sharper awareness of mundane failures in updating our social institutions and the optimism to overcome them. teamwork is the key, and our Space programs show that far-flung teamwork can be an everyday reality.

Our grievous shortcomings in the area of social institutions may be found also in a less familiar field: our treatment of Earth itself. Let us return for a moment to our allegorical fish. Having once attained the magical gift of travel through an alien element, they would surely keep using it (as we have done for some years now with our gift of Space flight), and in so doing they would just as surely change their way of thinking about their native element. Their fishbowl would look quite different from outside. As Father John Culkin of Fordham says, "We don't know who discovered water, but we're pretty sure it wasn't a fish." We never really discovered Earth until we got outside it.

To change the metaphor, throughout human history we have been tiny creatures infesting the body of a giant. Little by little we studied the pores and the hairs of the giant, but we could never see him whole. And we never wondered about his health. Now we see the vast body. We see poisons working in it. We see wounds and sores. We begin to understand the metabolism that used to keep it healthy; and we see that the self-correcting and self-protecting systems are breaking down.

We caused all this. Space satellites show us the full extent of the damage we have done to the giant and the consequent dangers that threaten him and us. These deadly dangers may soon be mankind's most urgent of all problems.

A major advance in civilization, as Alfred North Whitehead said, is a process that all but wrecks the society in which it occurs. The wrecking is all too evident wherever we look. Our society, still attuned to ancient rhythms of learning slowly and changing slowly, must now speed up to survive. Look back again at history. We were in this predicament once before. In medieval times, all the peoples of Europe got into the middle-aged habit of assessing old gains, counting the costs, and rejecting the new. They relaxed and turned off.

The great voyages of exploration awoke us and prodded us into the Renaissance. We moved ahead into the machine age. But the spread of change was slow. Few people noticed that the green places were vanishing, that the new smokestacks and airports and expressways were bordered by rotting old slums and thickening clots of hostile humanity.

Most of us firmly believed that the new sciences would make us richer—as indeed they have, in many cases—and happier, which remains in doubt. Our civilization went on blindly like a tractor, laying down its new road in the very act of removing the old one, no matter how it debased human lives and social institutions and the "good Earth" we had inherited.

Poets are often the first to show men what is happening. Here are a few lines from an unpublished poem written recently by Joe Weston:

> We are there, or just about.

> For how many years, thousands?
> have we spent our minds on making things.
> Objects of commerce, mostly.

> Apathy can drown us now.

Starting now, we meet each other's needs
or we're through, all of us.

And God might say, afterward,
looking at the dust we had become,
I offered them love, and they turned me down.
I wonder if I should try again?

Suddenly an old question from the Bible echoes in our ears:
"What is a man profited, if he shall gain the whole world and lose
his own soul?"

The feats of the rocket men have ripped off social blinders. We
are struck by the contrast between our godliness in Space and our
selfish squalor on Earth. We wonder, "What is our nation profited,
if we can rise up to the stars yet cannot conquer poverty here—
if we have no open space to enjoy, no woods to roam in, nothing
within driving distance except concrete, ghettos, KEEP OUT signs,
and crowds of strangers? What do we gain from our vaunted inventiveness?"

So the soaring rockets bring our eyes back to Earth, to long-
ignored old problems. This is one of those rare moments like the
Renaissance when the mentality of an entire people is going
through tremendous upward lift. Is it too much to hope that man
is in the process of developing a new world-consciousness that can
eventually lift him above the strife and filth he no longer ignores?

It is startling to see how our increasing power over nature has
cast us into deepening despair about ourselves. Dramatists, novel-
ists, folk singers, young dropouts, and revolutionaries keep howling
that man is sick, God is dead, life is meaningless and a kind of
bad joke. They see no point in seeking salvation by any means
except violence and the convulsions of lust. For the rest of us,
their uproar may be a warning that in the end all depends on improving the quality of our relationships with each other. To treat
one's neighbor as oneself today is not merely virtuous but a
desperate necessity.

In most ages the arts have been hopeful and creative, while the men of action grappled in the mud. But in our age, mathematics and astrophysics and optics and medicine are moving up toward newer worlds while most artists and scholars (and perhaps many churchmen?) are in retreat. Einstein and von Braun map the heights from which the universe can be seen, while Samuel Beckett buries his characters to their necks like rotting heads of cabbage and proclaims the age of the antihero.

Once free from the stupor of medieval times, every age but ours had its New World, its Northwest Passage or Wild West or Klondike to lure the mettlesome into the unknown and to inspire a surge of energy among even the stay-at-homes. These past three generations have sorely needed new mental and emotional horizons. At last Space is opening such vistas. We are struggling toward them. But our society is so interlocked that no one segment can advance alone. We can only move by helping each other—which is difficult.

But at least Westernized man no longer feels scarred and embittered and antiheroic. He will not drop out and turn off. He is kicking up his own storms, and he knows it. Surely that is good.

He is willing to dare against dangerous odds and even against reason—to reach for the moon. The Space program may possibly provide the mighty stimulant necessary to set in motion enough enterprise to end poverty, and the planning and coordination that may yet bring peace.

Once again, life is striving to make itself something better, to see the mind-blinding Space beyond the sky. Although it can no more comprehend Space than a fish comprehends land, it has begun floundering up to it anyway. We must pray that the inventiveness and pluck that enabled man to make nature a servant instead of an enemy will enable him to do the same for his own nature. The room for improvement within each of us is so great that Jesus named it the kingdom of God within man. This may be the deepest meaning of the Space Age.

2

WHY EXPLORE?

●

*Human culture has never been advanced (nor, in fact, have
the human problems of the poor been solved) by dispirited
civilizations inhibited by fear of the bold action that seeks
to achieve ever-increasing scope and purpose for life, wider
range for freedom.*

—John Cardinal Wright

●

Anyone who has wondered what it was like to live in the days that
followed Columbus' voyage is now finding out. Then, as now,
thoughtful men disputed the wisdom of faring into the unknown,
argued that the possible benefits could not justify the cost, warned
that the hazards were grave. And then as now the insatiably
curious, the venturesome, the young in heart pushed on anyhow.

The Space effort appeals to a great many people (though not
a majority, as polls have shown in the past few years) for many
reasons. Likewise, despite the sober money minded explanations
by economists, the widespread excitement about voyages into the
unknown during Europe's first Age of Exploration had little con-

nection with Europe's need for new trade routes or with the ready market for spices from the Indies. The vigor of the response to the challenge of exploration was out of all proportion to the prospective wealth to be gained.

The urge to explore goes much deeper than any intellectual considerations. The roots are biological. To see the driving power behind the great sagas of exploration—of both past and present— we must look far, far back. Evolution is the greatest success story in all eternity. The epic of the germinal seed, passed on through endless generations, always driving a few creatures to keep climbing and spreading and diversifying through hundreds of millions of years, is beyond the imagination of any romancer.

How much information is needed for the full specifications of even the simplest single cell? According to Fred Hoyle, an eminent mathematician and astronomer, the information that must be stored in one living cell is more than designers need for a nuclear reactor or an oil refinery; more, perhaps, than is needed to make a star.

Yet all its voluminous blueprints, all its finely detailed programs for development, its step-by-step instructions for operating itself and reproducing itself and manufacturing its own nourishment from materials nearby and then converting this nutrition into growth—all these are compressed into a library no bigger than a few ten-millionths of an inch. That library is nucleic acid, or DNA as it is familiarly known. Today's computer programers wish they could instruct their computers as efficiently as God instructs each living cell.

The eternal mystery about cells is that so many of them have been driven by a blind urge to move beyond their own comfortable environment. In reproducing themselves, they somehow bequeathed their children a set of invisible charts that enabled them to shape themselves differently and to specialize in various ways. So the primitive one-cell organisms multiplied and at last formed a more complex organism than a Space ship: man.

Man's supreme discovery in all the eons was not fire, not tools, but the human self. Early man, the half-animal, was poignantly aware of his imperfection and aloneness. With silence and mystery behind him and ahead of him, he heard gay little songs in his head and began to give voice to them. On his cave walls he painted animal pictures that would outlive him. He learned to laugh. He learned to love and to cherish. He learned to live in comparative harmony with others of his kind and to make plans for the common good. And always he was trying to become something better.

The practical people formed tribes. In their villages, similarities were more respected than differences. Strangers and eccentrics were not welcome. Yet while the tribes grew more and more comfortable and safe, a few odd characters kept leaving the beaten path, breaking off to go as strangers into strange places, for no practical purpose. It was just that they longed to see what was out there— even on high mountain peaks and barren icebound islands.

In some of the settled places, a mental ferment kept working. From the earliest prehistory, men gazed at the night sky and wondered. Before writing was invented, men named the celestial bodies and bowed down to images of the sun and moon. Astronomy became, probably, the first pure science. Its students patiently charted the wheeling of the constellations, the tiny daily dislocation in the sun's rising and setting, the slow waxing and waning of the moon. As usual with knowledge, their data eventually turned out to have mundane uses. The stars told the passage of the nighttime hours, so that nocturnal toilers and travelers could estimate how long the darkness would last. Endless nights of watching, generations of careful counting, eventually gave herdsmen and farmers a reliable guide to future events: they knew when to plant, when to prepare for harvest, when to expect colder or warmer seasons. The rising of the star Sirius at a certain spot in the eastern sky meant that rivers were about to flood. The fact that one star, Polaris, never moved gave seafarers and wandering traders a signpost that told direction. Without astronomy people would still be mistaken today about the nature of our Earth and its place among the heavenly bodies.

Poets and mystics were always ahead of the technicians in thinking of new worlds to conquer. The psalmists were directing men's gaze to the depths beyond the stars while the down-to-earth technicians were busy with the workings of the wheel, the lever, and the ox. Seeing birds, idlers talked of soaring up where they could look down like the birds and see a whole valley in one glance, or glide far away; Greek storytellers made legends of Daedalus and Icarus while technicians were shaping pillars and fundaments. So too was Ayer Katsi, the flying man, a legend among the hardworking Incas, to say nothing of the flying carpet of the Arabians and the angels of Christianity. Roman satirists, likewise, were writing fantasy journeys to the moon while technicians built galleys. The musician Vivaldi rode in imagination among the planets and composed the music of the spheres before scientists found the energy in steam kettles.

In the Dark Ages the search for knowledge all but died out. The world's great cultures were ingrown, insulated by geography or deliberate choice. India was caste-bound, China was complacent and bureaucrat-ridden, Japan had sealed its borders, Islam scorned infidels, Central and South America were ruled by grim priest-kings. Europe was a flat, cramped, disheartened, warring village glaring inward at itself. By the time of Columbus, the Europeans saw themselves as tired and decrepit, doomed to poverty and sickness. The famous *Nürnberg Chronicle* of 1493 predicted: "Conditions will be so terrible that no man will be able to lead a decent life."

Here is how the famous historian Samuel Eliot Morison describes that period, in his life of Christopher Columbus.

At the end of the year 1492 most men in Western Europe felt gloomy about the future. Christian civilization appeared to be shrinking in area and dividing into hostile units. For over a century there had been no important advance in natural science, and registration in the universities dwindled as the instruction they offered became lifeless. Institutions were decaying, well-meaning people were growing cynical or desperate, and many intelligent men, for want of something better to do, were endeavoring to escape the present through studying the pagan past.

Mr. Morison wrote that in 1942. As we reread it now, it seems to throw an eerie light on current troubles he could hardly have foreseen. And let us see what happened soon afterward.

Even as the *Nürnberg Chronicle* was turning readers' minds to an impending end of the world, a lonely caravel scudded before a winter gale into Lisbon with news that was to give old Europe another chance. Columbus had sailed to a New World and came back to tell about it. No one huddled on the shore that day could have guessed what consequences would flow from that voyage, any more than today's wisest men can foresee what the moon flight presages. But even in the slow tempo of the fifteenth century, dramatic changes came swiftly. Here is part of Mr. Morison's description.

The church, purged and chastened by the Protestant Reformation, puts her house in order; new ideas flare up throughout Italy, France, Germany and the northern nations; faith in God revives and the human spirit is renewed.

The change is astounding. A new world view has begun, and people lay plans for a golden age in the near future.

For two centuries and more, European expeditions with their few seamen would sail unfamiliar waters all over the globe. The open ocean was to those men what Space is to astronauts today—except that the seamen knew less about where they were going, had fewer hopes of returning, and faced fears that would not seem foolish until human knowledge had advanced much further.

Yet Christianity was an optimistic and expansionist religion, the one most encouraging to men of action. Men may well have had faith that God would protect them as they followed the old, dangerous lure of unknown seas and unknown shores. Or perhaps the crewmen did not consciously reason out their motives; there were mysterious lands to be found beyond the trackless sea—and mystery has a strange excitement for bold, observant, curious types who have kept mankind faring forth. Whatever the reason, ship after ship was able to find crewmen.

May it not have been simply the old primal instinct in our blood that sustained the Age of Exploration and settled the Americas? When the great blue voids call and the vast unknown wilderness beckons, if a man has that thing in his blood he can no more settle down than could the first creatures who struggled up from the comfortable prehistoric sea.

The instinct broke out like an epidemic among the homebodies as well as the explorers. Imaginations were mightily stirred. Great adventures in thought began. It was the age not only of Columbus and Magellan, Drake and DeSoto, but also of Leonardo, of Shakespeare, of More's *Utopia* and Galileo's telescope. The suffocating humdrum sameness of the medieval mass culture gave way to the glorious variety of the Renaissance. Man rediscovered himself.

In the long view, the poor of Europe were better served by the explorers than would have been the case if Europe's governments had resolved to use all available funds for a direct attack on poverty. The tremendous resurgence of mind and spirit lifted millions of men out of the mud and gave them a new dimension for growth.

And it seems significant, too, that the most advanced civilizations of the Americas—those of the Aztecs and Incas—were the most vulnerable to the brash reckless explorers. Once those great empires had been penetrated by Spanish arms, their autocratic administrative systems could be taken over entirely. The fatalistic natives, shunning exploration, used to order and obedience, served their new masters like crude machines. Wherever the explorers went they found peoples too confused or too indifferent to oppose them.

Down the ages there have always been those with dried-up

imaginations who asked, "What's the good of it? Why do you waste your time and money?" whenever they saw someone pursuing knowledge unrelated to any prospect of profit. Often no answer is at hand. But usually an answer eventually appears. Michael Faraday, playing with magnets and coiled wire, made odd discoveries that seemed totally useless. He was asked in Parliament what the value of electricity was, and he retorted, "Some day you will tax it." Of course he was right in the end.

Sir Isaac Newton, whose pure abstract thought was to change the whole course of science, was a grave man who is said to have laughed only once in his life. The laugh came when someone asked him what use in life Euclid's geometry was.

What has anyone gained from studying the cosmos all these centuries? The stars shone for at least five billion years before Earth was born. Presumably they will continue to shine and radiate for billions of years after man as we know him is gone. Nothing we learn, nothing we do, can change those stars. Can knowledge of them change us?

To a practical man, we can now give some practical answers that were not evident a few generations ago. The basic laws of Newtonian mechanics, without which the machine age could never have dawned, were evolved from astronomical observations. Likewise, one famous equation has been used to describe not only the stability of the solar system but also the electric field around a charge of electricity and the steady distribution of heat in a casserole under a broiler. And the basic concepts that enabled us to pluck a giant's power from the heart of an atom were developed by Einstein and others from observations of stars and planets.

Now, in order to land men on the moon, it is necessary to predict the exact effects of the ever-changing gravitational pulls of Earth, moon, and sun on the hurtling rocket ship. What began as an idle study of the heavens has taken man beyond the Earth, and has sent his obedient vehicles to many parts of the solar system. They are bringing us a rich harvest of benefits, as will appear in following chapters.

But man does not peer into the unknown in search of prosaic monetary gain. He does it because of the old unconscious need to stretch his soul by reaching out for the fabulous and puzzling. We have moved from the concept of a universe built around man by God, for man's benefit, to one in which man and Earth are the merest motes in an unimaginably vast creation. Likewise we have moved from a suspicion that we were the only intelligent beings in the universe to a near certainty that thinkers are alive in many, many far worlds, though they seem likely to remain forever unreachable by us. Recent detailed studies have led to an estimate by the Rand Corporation that there are about 640,000,000 Earth-type planets whirling around their own suns in "our" galaxy—planets so much like Earth that on them we might well step out of a Space vehicle, take a deep breath of oxygen-rich air, and look up at a blue sky.

Ten times as many galaxies inhabit our known Space as there are men on this teeming planet. As we ponder such numbers, must we not suspect that much of the life in the universe is equal to us in intelligence, or superior, simply because our kind came out of the caves such a relatively short time ago?

Closer to home, astronomers keep uncovering new questions that tantalize us: questions to which we may find answers in the new age of exploration that has just begun. Where do planets come from? What impels them to form? When and how does life begin on them? We don't know why Earth alone of our sun's planets has oxygen in its atmosphere, or why Earth is the only one of the inner planets with oceans, or why the moon is so big in relation to Earth. We don't know why little Phobos, the inner moon of Mars only ten miles across, registers on our instruments as being a thousand times lighter than that much water would be; if the figure is correct, Phobos must be a hollow shell, which has led Dr. I. S. Shlovskii, an eminent Soviet mathematician, to speculate that it may be an artificial satellite parked in orbit by Space explorers a few million years ago. Nor can we be dead sure that the innermost of Jupiter's twelve satellites is not a giant spacecraft left there by somebody some time.

We don't know why the huge planets farther from the sun are so much lighter, for their size, than are Mercury, Venus, Earth, and Mars, the planets closest to the sun. We wonder why Jupiter is so enormous; if Mars were placed on the face of Jupiter, it would look like a dime on a dinner plate, and one of its moons is actually bigger than the smallest planet. We wonder why the outermost planet of all, Pluto, resembles the inner planets more than it does its closer neighbors.

Such questions may seem remote from our everyday life. Yet the little we have learned about the atmosphere of Mars has begun to help us with long-range forecasts of Earth's weather. And what we have learned by study of comets and meteorites has told us something about ourselves and the surface of our own planet; we know that uncounted billions of micrometeorites hit Earth every day, adding more than two million tons of matter to the globe each year. Much of what the farmer plows is ancient star dust, milled and mixed for millennia by the wind and rain. And we too are the stuff of stars, for at the nuclear core of each molecule of human blood is an atom of the same iron that comes hurtling down in meteoric form from stars long extinct. Moreover, every atom on Earth has a spinning structure like that of our solar system with its circling planets.

We cannot foresee the practical benefits that will come from today's scientific research. But we can be sure that as long as men are born with questioning minds and access to mankind's great storehouses of accumulated knowledge, they will go on asking new questions of the universe, evolving new theories, and further enlarging our storehouses.

In the year 1969, after ages of dreaming about doing it and several millennia of writing the dreams on paper, the human family has begun sending couriers from solar planet number three to the globe of glowing rock called Luna. That globe's name had been given long ago to "lunatics" to describe those whose brains were smitten with crazy thoughts of far voyages. Suddenly the moon is no longer just a beautiful light in the sky. Now it is a place.

"What good is the moon?" people ask with an eye to the dollar. The scientists can only retort in answer, "What good is a baby?"

Nobody knows yet what good the moon will be to us. We shall consider many possibilities in various chapters of this book. But it is already becoming evident that the moon will be good *for* us. It is giving us back some of the confidence we had five hundred years ago, an exciting sense that we can keep learning. We are long past the days of the dragon boats and the glorious howl and lash of the spindrift in a man's teeth. But we have opened a door to the future, as they did. Just as the fifteenth century seamen started an irresistible tide of exploration, so will our Spacemen go on to other planets and perhaps to stranger places.

In the mid-1960's, philosophers and social workers talked and worried endlessly about the problems of spiritual poverty and urban decay. "We need something, and we need it quick," a speaker told intellectuals from twenty countries who gathered at Princeton in 1968. He warned of "the increasing divergence between what intellectuals do and think and what ordinary people are doing and thinking." There had been just such a divergence in the dreary medieval times. And for decades in this century there has been, as Santayana described it, "a sore of self-hatred and self-contempt; a wild throwing for something different, and a deep, dark impulse to destroy everything."

But in the late 1960's mankind's achievements in Space began to catch up with science fiction. It now seems clear that we of the later twentieth century are entering the most splendid chapter of the long epic of man's dogged determination to explore the universe and know the unknown. We go now to leave the Earth that gave us birth.

Are we ready for that chapter? Man has never been ready for

any forced march in his wild history. Yet most of the time he has kept on the move. This creature who dreams and prays himself toward humanity is alternately shocked and delighted as he sees his surroundings become ever more perplexing and challenging.

Our new, vast, complex, crowded, dirty, warring cosmopolis that was the world before Saturn-Apollo, has much in common with the world that was Europe before the Renaissance. On the face of it, Space flight has no more relevance to the problems and agonies of the world than the voyages of Columbus had to the ills of Europe. It is possible to glower at the moon over a Harlem rooftop and feel only bitterness at the money spent, the vast effort channeled, in exploration that may not improve a single tenement in the ghetto. And yet Space travel is the single greatest step in the single greatest age in history. The event is incalculable in its consequences, but somehow most of us sense that it will be good for all of us. As Hubert Humphrey said in 1967, "I think a certain extravagance of objectives—a will to push back the frontiers of the unknown—is the test of a vital society, a nation that intends to meet the challenges of tomorrow with a running start."

The triumphs of Apollo underline the irony that it is easier for man to go to the moon than to wipe out a slum, easier for him to coast through Space than to clean up his own polluted skies, easier for him to manage cooperation in a vast technological enterprise than to forge brotherhood in a city block. Yet as man has conquered the seas, the mountains, and the air, he has also at each stage, in a small way, conquered part of himself. Therein lies the hope and the ultimate promise of his conquest of Space.

3

CAN YOU IMAGINE?

●

*The universe is not only stranger than we imagine, it is
stranger than we can imagine.*

—J. B. S. Haldane

●

This century's last quarter is likely to be an age of exploration such
as man has never imagined before. Various educated guesses have
been made as to the timetable. Wernher von Braun, the famed
German rocket genius who now heads NASA's Space Flight
Center, laid out this forecast in 1967.

In the early 1970's, extended lunar exploration, with astronauts
fanning out across the face of the moon for weeks at a time;
Earth-orbit flights lasting three months. In 1973, soft landings
on Mars by two Viking robots with TV cameras and delicate
sensors. In 1975, the planets will be so placed that a Mariner

sailing past Venus will be swung by Venusian gravity into a course near Mercury, giving man his first closeups of the sun's nearest neighbor. In 1978, planetary positions will enable a craft approaching Jupiter to whip around past Saturn, Uranus and Neptune and perhaps land a small piggyback satellite. By 1982 a crew of nine astronauts can land on Mars, if the government decides early in the 1970's that such a goal is desirable. In the 1980's we may dig out a lunar base for 18 to 24 men; it could be big enough for 100 colonists at the turn of the century. (One odd thought in this connection: Children born up there, having been shaped by lunar gravity, can never come down here to the Old World; their muscles and bones would not be adapted to the sixfold increase in gravity.)

By the year 2000 we will undoubtedly have a sizable operation on the moon, we will have achieved a manned Mars landing and it's entirely possible we will have flown with men to the outer planets.

A more optimistic schedule is laid out in a 1964 book by two Russian government scientists named Bubnov and Kamanin.

By 1968-70, landing a man on the moon.

By 1972-75, establishing a 30-50 man Space station.

By 1975-80, manned flyby missions to Mars and Venus.

By 1980-90, landing a man on Mars.

These dates are speculative and only approximate the real possibilities. However, one must not forget that the successes of Soviet cosmonautics often outstrip the most optimistic prophecies of distinguished scientists and technologists.

Bubnov and Kamanin may have been remembering an ill-received prophecy of seven years earlier. At an October 3, 1957 meeting of the National Science Foundation in Washington, to discuss plans for the International Geophysical Year, some Soviet scientists mentioned a possibility of satellite launches in the near future. Most American scientists then regarded satellites as comic-book fantasies. Those in the distinguished audience who chuckled aloud had no way of knowing what the next day would bring. On October 4 the world was electrified by an announcement from the Kremlin: Sputnik I, the first satellite in all history, had been launched and was orbiting Earth.

How can it hang up there? wondered skeptics. They still "knew" that what goes up must come down. Of course they also knew that the moon hangs in the sky, and Sir Isaac Newton had explained why. But they did not realize that artificial satellites would obey the same great natural law as do the planets circling the sun and the moons circling the planets.

All bodies attract one another. Even two one-pound weights, a foot apart, have been proven to attract each other with a force of a half-billionth of an ounce. They obey the general law of universal gravitation, which Newton deduced in 1687. (Asked why Newton's strange law works, scientists can only shrug. It so happens that a Creator decreed it.) But the farther two bodies are from each other, or the smaller they are, the weaker their pull on each other. If they are moving, their motion helps them resist the pull.

Were it not for this pull, a bullet shot from a gun could theoretically go on in a straight line forever (except for the slowing by air friction) and the moon actually would sail through infinity in a straight path (since in Space there is no air to slow it). A bullet gradually sinks below the straight line along which it was fired, and it sinks just as fast as it would if you simply dropped it vertically. Thus, if the bullet hits a wall, the distance below its original horizontal firing is exactly the distance the bullet would have dropped straight down starting from rest, in the time spent between leaving the gun and hitting the wall. Gravity pulls it down in both cases.

This simple iron law also rules the moon. Its motion is like a bullet fired horizontally. At every moment, instead of moving indefinitely along the straight line on which it was fired, so to speak, it falls slightly toward Earth. It is perpetually falling toward us at a speed of .053 inch per second. But its high speed, about 2,300 miles per hour, is just enough for Earth's gravitation, weakened by distance, to hold it in orbit like a ball whirled on a string. (If a string breaks, the ball flies off in a stright line. The pull of gravity is a string that never breaks.)

Astronomy has proved the universality of this pull beyond doubt. Einstein theorized that even light rays bend toward the sun as they pass it; delicate measurements of starlight showed he was right.

Gravity holds us on the ground and brings us back if we jump upward. Fire a bullet straight upward, and the pull of Earth will gradually slow it until it comes to a momentary halt and then falls back. Dreamers began to wonder long ago if there is any limit to upward motion, and whether a projectile must necessarily stop and fall back whatever its starting speed. The answer would be yes if the force of gravity were the same all the way up. But gravity weakens slowly with height. In its upward motion an object loses a little less speed every second, rising a little farther than it would if gravity were just as strong up there. So the dreamers wondered whether, by leaving fast enough, it could manage never to fall back again.

Finally they calculated that a rocket fired up at a starting speed of 6.98 miles per second will never come back. This, then, is Earth's "escape velocity." The speed needed for escape from any celestial body can be computed from its mass and size. From the moon, it is only 1½ miles per second. This is why the small engine in Apollo's little lunar ferry can get two astronauts up off the moon's surface and back into orbit.

But the density of air is enough to melt down any object traveling faster than five miles per second, through the heat of friction. Even the solid rock of a meteorite is seldom large enough for much of it to be left by the time it gets down to Earth. This fact made it perfectly obvious to "practical" scientists that we could never fire anything into Space without burning it to a cinder en route.

The Space enthusiasts solved the problem by building multi-stage rockets that would start up very slowly and increase their speed very gradually, firing their second stage and perhaps a third at such heights that the boost would be much more powerful than at ground level. Putting a body in orbit around Earth is a balancing act. The centrifugal force due to the body's speed in its path around Earth must exactly balance the force of gravity at the body's distance from Earth. When such a balance is achieved, the body is in a stable orbit. The body and everything in it, or on it, or with it, is in a state of seeming weightlessness. If the body were to stop moving, it would fall to Earth in response to gravity. The calculations needed to put an artificial satellite into orbit are enormously laborious, but modern electronic computers can do them in a few moments.

In 1957, as Sputnik winked its derisive way across our skies each night, a national magazine polled leading American aerospace engineers and scientists on their expectations of future progress in Space. Their consensus was that man might somehow go up into Space by 1970 and might reach the moon by 1990. Actually, of course, man got into Space and hurtled around the Earth in 1961. Man reached the moon in 1969. As Lt. General Bernard A. Schriever, head of the Air Force's Systems Command, later said, "Historically we have tended to overestimate what we could do on a short-time basis, and to grossly underestimate what we could do on a long-term basis."

Robert Hotz knew all this history, as long-time editor of *Aviation Week and Space Technology*. Yet as recently as October 9, 1967, he wrote: "It is obvious now that neither the U.S. nor the USSR will land men on the moon before the end of this decade."

Three years after we entered Space, we were launching hundred-foot satellites. Three years after that we were orbiting a hundred spacecraft a year. The Space Age itself is just entering its teens. When it is in its twenties, what may we not be doing? Part of our difficulty in imagining what the next few years may bring is that change keeps coming faster and faster. The older we are, the dizzier we feel as the world of our boyhood disappears. This was not true in other centuries; change was rare and slow.

Think of it: the technology perfected in prehistoric times served in everyday life until the beginning of the nineteenth century. Even in the United States, city people lived in 1800 A.D. very much as city people had lived in 3000 B.C. Then with the opening puffs of the Steam Age, one country after another began to industrialize—each faster than its predecessors. England spent two centuries bring its industry to today's level. The United States took off from England's vantage point and achieved the same results in one century. The Soviet Union accomplished in fifty years what had taken us twice as long, because it could use technology already developed elsewhere.

New countries come in where others already are, not where they started. Japan did not start flying with the Wright brothers' biplanes but with the Zero types. Israel has never flown anything but jets. China came into the world of industrialization after transistors, computers, and atomic fission were available, so she may leap to industrial parity with the West in another decade.

The time lag between a dramatic scientific discovery and its widespread use has been shortening steadily. In 1831 Faraday made an experiment that was to change human history: he showed how to generate electricity. But nobody did much with it until Bell and Edison came along in the 1870's to start the billion-dollar telephone and electric utility industries. The automobile waited forty years for Henry Ford. But the first aircraft factories started only fourteen years after Kitty Hawk. Television took only ten years to get into factory production. The first atomic power plants were built just seven years after the first nuclear chain reaction at the University of Chicago. We were using satellites for communication only five years after Sputnik I.

It took man more than a million and a half years to fly off the surface of the Earth, and more than half a century to rise past the few miles of atmosphere. Less than ten years later, he is on the moon. Is it so hard to imagine he will soon be on other heavenly bodies?

Even now, when Space travel is a fairly familiar fact, many people wonder why scientists should fritter away time on such a frivolous, useless hobby. What is the good of Space to us on Earth? The full answer lies hidden in the mists of the future. Many partial answers will appear later in this book. But once again it is worthwhile to reflect on historical parallels.

What could seem more pointless, in earlier days, than peering at the stars? Many of us may remember our own reaction in school when we were shown how to estimate the inner temperature of distant stars: ingenious, but why should anyone want to know?

Yet astronomy produced the precise measurements that gave us calendars and clocks. It made possible the navigation of ships, planes, and Space vehicles. Fusion of atoms to produce energy was observed on the sun before we learned how to do it on Earth. Long ago, astronomy freed man from superstition and fear. Today, without basic knowledge of the behavior of distant stars, we would not be placing satellites in orbit.

The indirect social consequences of scientific findings are even harder to foresee than their direct uses. Who would have guessed that steam engines would make cities grow enormously? Who could have predicted that automobiles would take mother out of the kitchen, or revolutionize the dating habits of young couples? Who could have imagined that (as we shall see in Chapter 8) the invention of the silk hat in Paris would cause the formation of many small lakes in America?

In the early days of the telephone, most people thought its expense would keep it forever in the realm of laboratory curiosities. So too with liquid hydrogen, the hard-to-produce fuel that now enables engines to propel Apollo toward the moon. We have not yet changed society on Earth very much as a result of all the satellites in the skies today. But big changes are now within our power because of the satellites, and are on the way. Most chapters of this book will be concerned with them.

It is not inconceivable that some of nature's awesome powers, recently revealed, will enable us to reshape other heavenly bodies to suit our own needs. Biologists may be able to grow bacteria cultures that will consume the clouds of carbon dioxide on Venus, release oxygen, and ultimately change that planet's climate into one pleasant for man, with a breathable atmosphere. On Mars, with its weak gravity, great thousand-foot domes could be constructed and pumped full of air, so that men could work and play within them in light clothes.

If we do not find planets in an orbit that will sustain our life, we may try to tap the universe's storehouse of violent energy to push them into more satisfactory paths. We may even slow down or speed up their rotation to change the length of their seasons and days. Or we may construct new artificial planets of our own in the silent gulfs between the old ones. We may swing huge mirrors in controlled ellipses around Earth to reflect sunlight and thus prevent frosts, abate windstorms, and give the polar regions a mild climate.

Fantastic? Perhaps. But how fantastic would the thought have been of the Boeing 747, say, in the years when we rode the DC-3? How fantastic would the thought have been of the Apollo missions at the time of World War II?

Centuries ago men planted oaks that would take five hundred years to mature. They were able to think of the future and make preparations for it, in a way that is lost to us. Our minds seem rooted in the present. We have lost perspective on the past and future. We look for immediate payoffs. We seldom try to stretch our minds.

To demonstrate this, here is a simple mental exercise to try. Make an estimate of how many minutes have passed since the day Christ was born.

Probably you guess the total to be in uncountable trillions, don't you? Most people do. But even today, not many more than a billion minutes have gone by! With this new perspective on that vague word "billion," think of Space again and consider that astronomers now estimate there are 100 billion planetary systems in our galaxy alone. Or think of time and consider that Earth is known to be approximately five billion years old, while mankind has been a separate species here for only the last two million years. The slow, slow process of evolution from primitive creature to thinking human could repeat itself more than two thousand times during the time the Earth has existed, and can be repeated many more thousands of times during the coming billions of years that Earth will be inhabitable.

Sir James Jeans helps us visualize these time spans by asking us to imagine an obelisk the height of Cleopatra's Needle or the Washington Monument, with a penny on top of it and a postage stamp lying on the penny. The monument represents the age of Earth, the penny the whole age of mankind, and the stamp the length of time in which men have been even slightly civilized. The period during which life will still be possible on Earth corresponds to a further column of stamps perhaps a mile high. Think of this picture and imagine how much development may still be ahead of us. Man has scarcely begun his story.

The Space Age is expanding our consciousness far beyond its old limits. The young eagerly respond to this. The old find it harder. We have all seen this many times in very aged couples living alone in retirement, who have ceased to take in any new ideas from outside their own little circle. They feed back to each other the same thoughts day after day, making the same judgments, subconsciously resisting any change.

As we speed forward into an unknowable future, we must all be on guard against this subconscious resistance within ourselves. Psychologists and sociologists have begun to talk of a phenomenon they call "future shock," akin to the older phenomenon of "culture shock"—the disorientation that afflicts an unprepared visitor when he is plunged into a strange society. Peace Corps volunteers suffer from culture shock in a Liberian village or a Brazilian slum. Set down suddenly in an environment sharply different from his own, anyone may feel bewildered and frustrated.

The victim of culture shock can go home. Future shock is a worse dislocation, for the victim knows he can never return to what he has left behind. Time has altered everything beyond recognition. Future shock may deprive people of the ability to deal rationally with their new surroundings.

This is the threat we all face in the coming years. Most of us are psychologically unprepared to cope with continuous, complex, torrential change. Even the most educated people still live their lives in the unconscious assumption that society is relatively static. Children are taught to orient themselves toward fixed goals—to study hard to become a doctor or engineeer or priest, as their grandfathers were. Nobody stops to think that it is utterly impossible to conceive what "being a doctor" or anything else will mean two decades hence. No profession of the future will fit the molds into which we are trying to pour our children. The result is unreadiness to meet the future as it arrives: future shock.

What can be done to prepare ourselves and our children against this disability? For one thing, we should exercise our imaginations often and vigorously. We need to create a strong future-consciousness. Alertness toward all the conceivable social and personal implications of the future, as well as its probable technological leaps, can help give us the needed flexibility and mental youthfulness. To do this, we must habitually do more speculating about the future. We must stop assuming that such-and-such "can never be done." We must keep reminding ourselves of ridiculous-sounding proposals, such as those cited in this chapter, which proved to be turning points in civilization.

For another thing, we must retrain ourselves to be more aware of gradual changes as they occur. Our physical and nervous systems evolved primarily to react to sudden stimuli—the shadow of the swooping hawk, the baby's cry, the swerving automobile. We seldom notice long-term transformations. We tend not to perceive the aging of a daily associate, or the slowing of our own reflexes.

If the change from the Los Angeles of 1930 to that of 1970 had happened overnight, its residents would have resisted fiercely. But the slow forty-year change crept through the city almost unnoticed. Let us watch keenly for trends, and do something about them before they get out of control. Let us anticipate and manage change instead of merely reacting to it.

Our generation is the last to be imprisoned on one planet. We stand on the brink of the ocean of Space, preparing machines to take us into the greatest adventure in all history. Let us prepare our minds as well.

4

A NEW VIEW OF EARTH

●

We have succeeded in opening wide the door to outer space, and now we are turning around and looking back. We have made our Earth not just the springboard to space research, but the object of it.
   —Stewart L. Udall, former Secretary of the Interior

●

Not since the first explorers put out to sea has there been such a widening of man's understanding of Earth as in these first years of space exploration. But this new perspective has brought into sight a troubling question. Is one of Christianity's ancient beliefs a danger to mankind? At least one eminent historian thinks so. Dr. Lynn White, Jr., director of the UCLA Center for Medieval and Renaissance Studies, says "The roots of the increasing imbalance in nature are . . . deeply rooted in Christian theology. Our daily habits of action are dominated by an implicit faith in perpetual progress which was unknown either to Greco-Roman antiquity or to the Orient." The dire consequences of that faith, he thinks, "may annihilate us unless we find a new religion or re-think our old one."

On the other hand, *National Geographic* for January 1969 says that our new and fast-widening knowledge of Earth "offers a veritable cornucopia of benefits for the future of the human race." And as long ago as January 1964, *Fortune* reported that "the new knowledge acquired in space exceeds by far the value of funds so far spent."

This chapter and the next few will pursue these seemingly con-tradictory theological and materialistic lines of thought. We begin by looking at facts on which the hopeful materialist line of thought is based.

When most people speak of the Space effort they think of the programs for manned Space flight. Yet manned Space flight ac-counts for less than half the total effort devoted to heaving metal into Space. That total also includes at least ten distinct kinds of operating satellite that we have hung in the cosmos to serve our immediate needs here on the ground. Our new workaday super-servants, known as artificial satellites, are exposing Earth's secrets as never before. These man-made moonlets see or record what our own senses could never perceive. Often they measure what our finest instruments on the ground could never detect or analyze.

Out on the rim of Space, whirling silently around our planet at heights from 100 miles to 70,000 miles or more, are a wondrous variety of robot observers and messengers. They range from the early grapefruit-sized Vanguards to the later "flying boxcars" packed with miracles of electronic miniaturization—magnetometers, ra-diometers, radiation counters, scintillometers, infrared spectrom-eters, and the like. Some carry cameras that take recognizable photos of objects smaller than a Volkswagen from altitudes of 300 miles.

In the first eleven years of the Space Age some 800 spacecraft rocketed out from Earth. They sent back floods of data revealing that Space is not "empty" but laced with vast invisible forces and with matter in several strange forms. But they also revealed surprises on Earth—surprises that stimulated us to "step out and see" more of what our planet looked like from outside its hundred-mile-thick envelope of gases.

The artificial satellite is already considered as revolutionary a device as the telescope, which opened our windows on the universe and capsized ancient theologies. The strange sensory systems in satellites enable us to mount a continuous global survey of all the lands and seas. Not only have they given us accurate maps of heretofore inaccessible areas, but they are beginning to give us a far better understanding of world weather and how to predict it; a far fuller picture of the world's mineral, vegetable, and animal resources and what is happening to them day by day; a far finer worldwide web of communications; a new pattern of unvarying artificial stars by which navigators can steer more precisely in all weathers. And beyond these are newer uses we are just beginning to realize.

At this writing there are more than 400 man-made satellites in orbit and in touch with ground stations. They are harvesting so much new knowledge about Earth that the *Journal of Geophysical Research* has had to double its frequency and expand its size. Today weather forecasting is virtually dominated by data from Space; savings to the world economy achieved with satellites are already measured in billions of dollars; navigation by satellite is routine; communication relay by satellite is a fundamental and fast-growing part of international life; plans for strengthening world peace with inspection satellites are maturing; and the almost magical tools of photogrammetry, first put to wide use with aerial cameras, are being vastly extended with satellites.

The satellites' scrutiny of Earth is known as "remote sensing." Their sensors peer down with preternatural keenness to "see" the unseeable through darkness, clouds, smoke, dense vegetation, ice, or seawater, or tons of dirt. This is made possible by the strange but simple fact that basic units of energy called photons are forever radiating from every object in the universe.

These radiations travel in waves rather like those produced by a stone dropped in a pond. Their wavelength (distance from crest to crest) may be hundreds of miles for the longest, or about a ten-billionth of a centimeter for the shortest. Only a few of these waves are visible to us as light waves. Our eyes see through a narrow slit admitting about one-sixtieth of the total electromagnetic spectrum that can be "seen" by remote sensors in Space.

Clear across the visible and invisible spectrum, all objects emit waves of photons in distinctive "spectral signatures" written by the oscillations of the objects' atoms and molecules. As scientists build a memory bank to identify these signatures, they can tell not only what an object is but how old, how hot, how big, and how healthy it is. For example, the cells of a sick plant reflect or emit radiation differently from the way healthy cells do, even before the sickness is visible to our eyes—and telltale squiggles on streams of paper, recording the satellites' observations, can show us the unmistakable diagnosis.

As they coast in distant orbit, the new sensors can glance at a rock formation anywhere on Earth and send back a string of digits telling us the rock's mineral makeup. They can analyze the chemical content of soil so we can predict its fertility. They can distinguish the signature of a hardwood forest from a conifer forest; prime timber from insect-infested wood; poisonous weeds from harmless ones; polluted water from good water. They can trace ocean currents and warm-water pockets. They can locate dangerous icebergs and valuable schools of fish.

If we wish, they can bring back ghostly pictures of the past. Infrared photos taken over Nova Scotia show subterranean outlines of Acadian buildings razed when the settlers were deported in 1755; with the new-old charts, Nova Scotians are restoring the long-vanished structures. Similar photos have helped make the vast bleak badlands of Negev bloom as they did in biblical days. Infrared sensors located areas there that had borne rich crops. They delineated the old dams, canals, catchment basins and bridges that had made those lands cultivable in Roman and Byzantine eras. Although Negev's annual rainfall is only six inches

—all dumped in a few hours of flash floods—the farmers of two thousand years ago had produced bountiful yields by damming torrential streambeds and cutting irrigation ditches. Now Israel's government is duplicating the lost developments. A desert uninhabited since 450 A.D. is fruitful again.

This kind of knowledge and action, on a global scale, is urgently needed to ease the squeeze of impending worldwide food shortages. Already some four to ten million human beings starve to death each year, and at least half the people on Earth suffer from malnutrition or hunger. Worse yet, the Population Reference Bureau now reports that 324,000 babies are born every day somewhere in the world, while only 133,000 people die. Thus Earth acquires about 190,000 new mouths to feed each time it turns. In a year this is enough to populate France, Belgium, Holland, and a few smaller countries besides. The leaps in population are most rapid in those regions least able to feed them: the so-called underdeveloped nations of Africa, Asia, and Latin America. Unless the poorer nations can grow more food and make better use of other natural resources, these nations seem condemned to famine, pestilence, disorder, and bloodshed on a massive scale—with consequences for the rest of the world that are hard to estimate.

"Many millions of people are going to starve," Sir Charles P. Snow warned in November 1968. "We shall see them doing so upon our television sets. We shall, in the rich countries, be surrounded by a sea of famine unless . . . tremendous social tasks are [put into] operation." The tasks he listed included massive grants of food and technical aid from rich nations to poor and vast improvements in food production by poor nations themselves.

Such crucial tasks can be accomplished only if we hitch our farm wagons to our man-made stars, the satellites—if we link Space with agriculture. We are on the verge of doing so. By late 1970 a program called EROS (Earth Resources Observation Satellite) is expected to throw its first satellite into orbit as a joint effort of the Interior Department, the Agriculture Department, and NASA. Dr. William A. Fischer of the U.S. Geological Survey calls EROS

"the most valuable satellite or space program ever considered."
And Congressman Joseph E. Karth, chairman of the House sub-
committee on Space Science & Applications, has voiced his committee's belief that EROS "could represent the greatest direct
return on investment of any aspect of the space program."

The first EROS craft is planned to carry three special multi-
purpose television cameras into orbit 500 miles above us. These
cameras and other detectors (some so small that ten would fit in a
bee's eye) can flash data to computers trained to recognize patterns automatically. Put together, the satellite-sensor-computer
system can advise agriculturists where and when to plant; can
sweep its robot eyes over vast fields of grain and fruit, predict their
yields, and detect crop diseases early enough to save much of the
harvest. The system can "take the temperature" of a volcano and
warn when the core is heating up for an eruption. It can map
and measure snowpack distribution so accurately that the computer can foretell future effects on vital water supply, on erosion,
on dams and roads and drainage basins, and on many kinds of
insect, animal, and vegetable life.

Consider what this new view of Earth means to a geologist, a
farmer, a fisherman, a surveyor.

The oldtime geologist in hobnailed boots, chipping rocks with
a hammer or gratefully following excavation crews for a look at
underlying strata, is no longer earthbound. Unmanned satellites
can give him almost a God's-eye view of vast areas. Multispectral
photos from Space show him the unknown formations deep underground. Thus he can judge where to drill for oil and natural
gas, or for veins of valuable ore.

The geologist's new clairvoyance comes none too soon. The
world is running low on reserves of copper, lead, zinc, petroleum.
Even the rich natural storehouse of the United States is straitened.
America has used more minerals and fuels in the last thirty years
than the whole world did in all previous history—and our current
consumption of minerals will probably double by 1975.

Trying to inventory Southeast Asia's resources, the United Nations found 95 per cent of that area too blank on geological maps for a guess at its natural deposits. Vast other territories are just as vague. But if have-not nations are to get on their feet and off the foreign aid list, geologists must find their subterranean riches. EROS can guide them.

What of the farmer? Our grandparents knew all about their farm—where the soil was best for corn, where to graze the cows, which crops were doing well or poorly and why. They knew it as familiarly as they knew their family circle. Hence they could use land efficiently. With EROS, a government can know its hinterlands as thoroughly as a small farmer knows his farm, and can plan its agriculture even more wisely. Crops that look identical to a man walking through them are very different to infrared scanning. Saltiness of soil in Texas cotton fields showed clearly from photographs made in the Gemini program. Remote sensors can detect black stain rust, one of the worst crop diseases, several precious days earlier than can a farmer studying the plants with a magnifying glass.

Shipping fleets as well as fishing fleets can be routed more profitably with up-to-date information on what waves and currents are doing, what is happening to reefs and sandbars and shorelines, where the ice dangers are, how warm or how deep the water is. Remote sensors can "feel" ice on the Great Lakes and report where it is thinnest, or how soon it is likely to melt. They can take the temperature of distant sea water, accurate to half a degree. (Some sensors will register microwave emissions from an ice cube a mile away.) Such information, used to reroute a ship, may easily save it a half-day's voyaging now and then.

We need far-flung legions of highly efficient miners and farmers, and fleets of well-informed fishermen, in order to steal a march on world famine. Likewise we need roads in undeveloped lands. We need factories near them. We need dams for flood control and electricity. We need air strips, seaports, pipelines. But for all these improvements we first need the surveyor.

Without a good map, a region cannot be quickly opened up to

technology. The planners of change must know the contours; must be aware of streams and swamps and mountain passes; must avoid areas with high risk of earthquakes, landslides, crop diseases, pest invasions.

Until very recently, maps could be created only by surveyors who rode or clambered or waded over the terrain with steel tape and theodolite. This is why only 7 per cent of Earth's land surface has yet been mapped well enough to multiply its yields. Even in the United States, only 40 per cent of the land is adequately mapped. Surveyors are far behind in charting the changes wrought by forest fires, droughts, floods, erosion, pollution, and other shifts in nature's delicate balance.

But satellites give us the instruments to map the whole Earth and catalogue its unseen reserves in a matter of months. We have not yet done so, for financial and political reasons, but we have made a start and are gaining momentum. Mosaics of topographical maps are growing from the first full photos of the Himalayas and Andes brought back by Gemini IV and V. One Apollo photo of the Nile delta enabled cartographers to locate and label more than a thousand native villages that no map had shown.

We know that US forest fires cause havoc costing more than $450 million per year. Fighting the fires costs another $150 million. No one knows the intangible extra loss from harm to soil, water resources, wildlife. But now the total loss is shrinking because airborne sensors are used for instantaneous and exact mapping of firelines through dense smoke, and for charting the direction and speed of the fire's onrush.

Plant diseases and insects are worse destroyers than fire. If we can reduce crop loss by only 1 per cent in the United States, our gain in one year will be about $75 million. To ferret out infections and insects the Agricultural Research Service spends $3 million a year, the Forest Service $5 million. A remote sensing satellite can take the work off their hands for no more than $2 million, according to expert testimony in Congressional hearings. Aircraft now do some remote sensing and mapping. But an aerialphotography map of the United States would take three to ten years and 1,500,000 photos, and cost about $12 million. A satellite can make the map in 17 days with 400 pictures, and it would cost only $750,000.

Satellite maps and sensors can quickly add several billion dollars' worth of food to the world economy because they will mean less groping and guesswork in crop planning, harvest scheduling, pest control, and water-supply management. It is anyone's guess how many billions will also be added in new discoveries of oil, natural gas, and minerals. These are part of the "cornucopia of benefits" envisaged by *National Geographic*.

The benefits hold further implications for religion, as hinted at the start of this chapter. We may become rather suddenly and sharply aware of what St. Luke told us in the Bible, "Unto whomsoever much is given, of him shall be much required."

Man's ancient warfare with himself and with nature, a drama as fateful as the story of the Garden and the Fall, is entering a decisive new phase. That phase was perhaps foreseen two centuries ago by the philosopher Jean Jacques Rousseau, who warned, "You are undone if you once forget that the fruits of the earth belong to us all, and the earth itself to nobody." In the dawning Space Age, his words mean that the churches' concept of stewardship must now take on a wider meaning.

In order to consider the full religious significance of the Space scientists' glimpses of a global horn of plenty, we need also to know the enormous potential of one more kind of satellite they have created: the weather satellite. Strangely, in this age of technology, the primal forces of weather impinge more fiercely than ever on civilization's vast network of production and trade. Crops and herds still live or die by the weather. In an hour a tornado can ruin a town that took decades to build. Let rain become too rare and civilization sinks under the sand, as in Central Asia; let it become too plentiful and civilization chokes in jungle, as in Central America.

Losses to floods, storms, drought, and other bad weather are conservatively reckoned at about 1,200 lives and $11 billion a year in the United States alone. The National Academy of Sciences estimates that American farmers, builders, public utilities, and property owners can save $2.5 billion a year when they know what the weather will do a week or two in advance.

Forecasting the wind or rain or temperature in any given location for more than a day or two ahead is, as the late brilliant mathematician John von Neumann once said, as complex and difficult a mathematical puzzle as the human mind has yet attempted. Weather in a given area cannot be exactly predicted except as a part of the total behavior of the atmosphere. This behavior is influenced by an incredible variety of faint forces: the carbon dioxide spewed by chimneys; the energy from the sun's moody magnetic storms; the nitrogen hurled to the land by lightning, which strikes Earth somewhere about 100 times every second; the resistance to wind by landscape, suddenly stiffening when the trees leaf and underbrush comes up in spring; the number and weight of particles from disintegrated comets swept up by Earth in its rush through Space, piling more than two million tons of matter onto our planet's surface each year.

Mathematicians call such an intricate engine as the atmosphere a "complex system." Earth is about as complex as a system can be. The sun is far simpler mechanically. Even the universe is simpler. This is because nothing that happens on Earth can affect the sun. And nothing that happens in our sun can affect the galaxy of 100 billion suns in which it moves. But Earth's ultimate fate depends on the mathematically simple system of the universe and the mathematically simple evolution of our sun, so its fifty-billion-year destiny can be foretold with absolute certainty.

Its day-to-day future is far harder to determine. In fact, until men and instruments got off the ground to study the energy flow and the circulation patterns, weather forecasting was mostly guesswork from reading barometers and mapping air-pressure areas that wandered in unforeseeable paths.

In the 1950's von Neumann and a team of specialists at Princeton's Institute for Advanced Study began constructing a crude but comprehensive mathematical model or simulation of the atmosphere, using past weather records and aircraft observations of the skies. The equations and results improved steadily with trial and error. Eventually they enabled government meteorologists armed with a computer at Suitland, Maryland to predict the course of weather over large regions. Since 1966 they have whipped out two-day forecasts more accurate than one-day forecasts a decade earlier, even to predicting the probable volume of rain or snow.

Starting in 1960 with the first meteorological satellite Tiros (Television Infrared Observation Satellite), weathermen saw for the first time the majestic cloud and storm patterns they had been drawing on their maps. As ground stations received the first of several hundred thousand photographs to come from the Tiros series, the meteorologists realized that they had "gone from rags to riches overnight," as one of them said.

In 1967 alone the satellites enabled hurricane forecast centers to flash warnings of 61 different storms in this country and abroad. But weather satellites have many more uses than to warn of hurricanes: they carry instruments that measure leakage of heat out of the atmosphere—important data never obtainable before. They transmit hundreds of photos of Earth's cloud cover each day and night. They track the direction and speed of great swarms of insects in Asia and Africa, giving warning of the threat to crops. Early in spring they survey ice fields and predict when shipping can get through; this forecast alone saves Canada and the United States an estimated $1,700,000 each year.

The work begun by the sun-powered Tiros series has continued and expanded with the more advanced Nimbus and Essa (Environmental Science Services Administration) satellites, giving virtually global coverage and establishing the first worldwide weather forecasting system. Today any nation can set up, for a few thousand dollars, simple ground equipment to interrogate an Essa as it passes overhead and receive from it the weather picture for thousands of miles, on facsimile recorders like those used by wirephoto news services. Some 29 nations now do so.

Farther-out views of Earth and its atmosphere are visible through a camera hung motionless in the sky, 22,300 miles up. This camera is part of the new Applications Technology Satellite, in stationary orbit above the equator. The camera is a recently designed "spin-scan" device that actually spins 100 times a minute, taking line-scan pictures similar to but sharper than a television picture. Taken every twenty minutes, these superb full-faced color portraits of Earth are combined into speeded-up movies so that scientists can see the actual circulation of the atmosphere. They learn more from such movies than they might in years of ground-level study.

Weather experts need at least twice as much hourly data, and a supercomputer about a hundred times faster than the best now running, in order to make reliable week-long forecasts—and perhaps to explain still unsolved puzzles of the planet's weather mechanisms. For example, nobody knows why the oceans' oxygen content has thinned by about 12 per cent since 1920. Nor does anyone know what happens each spring when ocean levels drop eight inches throughout the northern hemisphere, without any equalizing rise south of the equator. Even with the new satellites, only about a tenth of the globe is yet under detailed weather watch. We lack reports on hour-to-hour conditions throughout the tropics, that hot and watery expanse which ferments many potent weather disturbances. To fill in blank spaces and help unravel the remaining riddles of the atmosphere, the World Meteorological Organization has marshaled a program called the World Weather Watch, paid for with funds committed by many nations.

Of course meteorologists cannot set up laboratory experiments to study the workings of weather. The best way to deepen their understanding is to deploy instruments across a big section of Earth and set up a laboratory as large as nature. They will do this, for 18 months starting in 1972, over two million square miles of the South Pacific. There will be similar studies in other areas during the following years. This World Weather Watch will also use at least four of the most advanced weather satellites now being developed, along with a few Essa-type satellites for closeups of smaller areas from polar orbits.

The ultimate system will also require a computer with speed and capacity greater than anything known so far. An engineering group at the University of Illinois is designing such a monster, to be built by Burrough Corporation, with the ability to multiply a hundred numbers together in a millionth of a second.

Once such a computer is working, sometime within the next ten years, it will be invaluable not only for forecasting but also for simulating attempts at weather control, to predict what their long-run overall results would be. "A vast array of experiments on weather modification can be 'performed' by numerical computation rather than in nature," says Walter O. Roberts, the director of the National Center for Atmospheric Research. "For example, a dam can be 'built' across the Bering Strait for an infinitesimal fraction of its real-life cost, and we can evaluate its effect on the Kamchatka or Canada wheat-growing season without actually taking the risk."

Attempts to influence weather must be approached thus cautiously, meteorologists agree, because otherwise the backlash could be unforeseeably far-reaching—even disastrous.

Man might learn to dispel dangerous hurricanes or steer them away from cities, but thereby he could inadvertently make them dump their rain at sea, parching the mainlands. Moreover, Italian meteorologist Giorgio Fea warns that tinkering with nature's colossal machinery might trigger "thermal imbalances so violent that even the great Biblical events would pale beside them." Because there is such a delicate balance between Earth's radiation and the energy it absorbs from the sun, a tiny change in the equation could conceivably bring on a new Ice Age or melt the polar ice caps to flood Earth's lowlands.

We must beware lest we misuse our shreds-and-patches theory of the world. In our planning we must reverse the order of ordinary scientific study: we must fix our mind on wholes first, parts second. We must think of Earth as a giant orchestra that must be kept in harmony. This is part of the great midcourse correction that is required of our civilization.

Nature's own product, man, now jeopardizes nature's stability on the planet. The satellites warn us unmistakably. We have been breaking up our dwelling to warm our bodies; we have been casting a pall over the world that may make it unlivable; we have avoided cooperating in a world so crowded that disharmony can destroy us all. Throughout history most people have lived out their lives heedless of the future or indeed of anything but their own selves and property. But this is an age unlike any other. The opening-up of Space has hastened the time for all the world's great religions to acknowledge the brotherhood of man, worldwide. It is the Christian hope that planetary unity in planning for our shared tomorrows will be speeded toward reality by the active involvement of religion. Otherwise we perish.

We must hurry to pull tentative programs like EROS and World Weather Watch out of politics and into the skies. We must make sure our robot whirligigs are used not selfishly to fatten a few rich and educated nations, but generously, so that the fruits of the earth will indeed belong to all mankind, as Rousseau reasoned that they rightfully should.

We must hurry to unlearn the dogma that God created everything in the world exclusively for men's benefit, to be reshaped or squandered at will. Perhaps St. Francis of Assisi was wiser than we know in his concern for the well-being of beasts and birds. Perhaps, as Lynn White suspects, the primitive reverence for nature was wiser than our haste to harness it for any whim.

The great lesson of the last few years is that natural resources and scientific devices must be administered in trust by our generation for the next. What specific acts will this require from each of us as individuals? Exactly what are the dangers if we neglect our stewardship? Exactly where and how are we falling short, as of now? These are the questions to which the next few chapters will address themselves.

5

CLUTTER IN OUR SPACE SHIP

●

The Earth has come largely under the control of a cul-
ture which traditionally sees man's proper role as domi-
nating nature, rather than living in harmony with it. . . .
Our first move must be to convince all those we can that
the planet Earth must be viewed as a space ship of limited
carrying capacity.
    —Paul R. Ehrlich, Stanford University biologist

●

Mankind has left the age of the "cowboy economy," as some
historians call it, and entered the age of the "Spaceman economy."

Until recently, civilization regarded water, air, and land as the
Indians did buffalo. There were always more, and nature cleaned
up whatever people spoiled. If a city grew too crowded, if the air
was smoky or the water bad, any venturesome souls could always
trek into the unspoiled wilderness and live by hunting or fishing
or farming.

Most of mankind can no longer do this. Our frontier has
vanished. The new "Spaceman economy" forces us to realize that
Earth, like our Apollo moonships, is a self-contained system,

automatically renewing itself yet ready to stifle us or poison us if we let the system get jammed. In a closed loop such as Earth or Apollo, only sunlight gets in; nothing gets out. Everything must be reconstituted and made useful again and yet again, endlessly. Therefore man must now fit himself carefully into the increasingly clogged system. He cannot live as heedlessly within it as cowboys did on the limitless plains.

What is to be done with millions of plastic containers that do not decay, cannot be sunk, cannot burn, do not break, and will not go away? What is to be done with nonreturnable glass bottles and aluminum cans that litter the land and are virtually indestructible by natural processes?

Americans junk more than six million old cars and trucks a year. Now that these are abandoned in big cities at the rate of one every half-hour in every city, and cost more to tow away than they are worth as scrap, what are the cities to do with them?

Each city dweller in the United States now discards some six to eight pounds per day of solid waste products—garbage, empty containers, newspapers, dead animals, grass cuttings, old machines and their parts—or about double the weight of forty years ago.

The sheer expense of the problem is painful to taxpayers. America spends more than $3 billion a year on refuse disposal—almost as much as it spends on Space exploration. Yet most cities face serious crises in "waste management" within the next twelve years. Recently a conference of planners at the University of Michigan heard an expert point out, "A brief interruption in the task of waste disposal, or failure to take into account the bigger task it will be tomorrow, could trigger epidemics and regional paralysis."

Burning trash pollutes somebody's air. Grinding it and flushing it away pollutes somebody's water. Most communities are fed up with this policy of "pollute thy neighbor." But no better policy is yet in wide use. The most enlightened of today's common disposal methods is to tamp down each day's load of refuse and cover it with earth to make new farmland, parks and athletic fields. Unfortunately this takes a lot of dirt and space—an acre piled seven feet high for every ten thousand people every year. New York City annually fills in some 200 swampy acres on Staten Island with wastes, and will use up its available landfill space by 1977.

Science and government have awakened to the threat. In 1965 Congress passed the Solid Waste Disposal Act, to develop new ways to convert our leavings into something useful. More than 100 research projects are underway. Eventually there are likely to be regional networks of long-distance pipelines through which all wastes can simply be pumped out of town. Already Sweden and Britain have pneumatic tubes that whisk bulk household refuse to central incinerators as much as two miles away.

We are beginning to realize that we need a vast new system of waste disposal: a system more versatile and flexible than a missile warning network or a telephone company, and just as important. The new art of systems design, cultivated by the aerospace companies, is likely to provide a waste disposal system as soon as taxing authorities agree on how to pay for it. Since waste disposal systems have been built for manned spacecraft, the problem of designing them for larger units does not look particularly difficult.

In the meantime, if long-haul transportation costs can be cut, cities can find ample room for their residue in abandoned quarries, in the holes of huge mining operations, and on other faraway barren land. Most freight cars enter a city full and leave empty. They could carry out wastes and use them to fill big cavities, for everyone's benefit.

So we see that various kinds of technology can help solve our waste problem. But technology will not be enough. New patterns of neighborliness must emerge—which will happen only when we, as citizens, demand them. So far, voters aren't excited about garbage or trash. Therefore political leaders aren't excited either. Governors don't put their gold plaques on landfills. In struggling with the garbage glut, neighboring communities often ignore each other. For example, an engineering firm worked out a cooperative plan for three Connecticut towns, whereby one town's foul-smoking, old-fashioned incinerator could be modernized for odorless use by all three towns, with the cost shared by all. Voters defeated the plan. They objected to helping pay for other towns' garbage.

This go-it-alone lunacy has begun to give way to common sense. For example, 70 separate municipalities within Los Angeles County have pooled their resources to organize one of America's best refuse-disposal systems. But countrywide or even regional systems will eventually be too small. Within a generation we shall have to face the fact that Earth is one interconnected system which must dispose of all its wastes cleanly and usefully or risk a global breakdown. The problem is bigger than any nation.

We shall also be cramped by a dangerous overload of passengers on Space Ship Earth. The United States population is forecast to grow by an average 1.3 per cent per year even if our total number of babies born each year continues to drop slightly, as it has in recent years. A yearly population growth of 1.3 per cent may seem tiny, but it is almost literally blotting out the land that most of us see. Each year bulldozers chew up a half-million acres of American soil for new factories, subdivisions, airports, and other works of man. Today Long Island is a sample of what may soon exist elsewhere; paving and buildings cover so much of it that part of the scanty remaining open land has to be fenced off for special sump pits, to collect rainwater so it can soak into the shrinking underground water tables.

When today's children reach middle age, they almost certainly will live in regions as teeming as Europe, with its 232 people per square mile, instead of the 60 we now average. Already the whole state of New Jersey has 807 people per square mile—twice the population density of India. And we add the equivalent of Los Angeles or Philadelphia to the population of our cities each year.

The rush to the swollen cities is not just an American problem. The whole world is urbanizing helter-skelter. Today city blight eats at forests and grasslands and farmlands in Africa, Asia, Latin

America. Within about thirty-three years half of all people will be city-dwellers, for they are no longer tied to the plow by the grim need to produce their own food.

Only the United States and nine other nations grow more food than they eat. All other populous countries, including China and Russia, must import more than they export.

For Americans to say "This is no problem of ours" is like telling a fellow passenger, "Your end of the ship is sinking." Why is overpopulation elsewhere a concern of Americans? For one reason, there will be danger to all mankind if the human population is left to stabilize itself in the automatic manner of the animal world: through mortal fights between groups, through degeneracy, through a drop-off in births due to stresses of over-crowding (one experimenter with rats calls these stresses "pathological togetherness"), through famine deaths, and through diseases stalking quietly among hordes weakened by malnutrition.

If such havoc arises, frantic mobs may do almost anything that might mean more food. Think of the abundance they have glimpsed among more fortunate people. Think of their hopelessness about their personal future. Is it surprising that firebrand agitators can sometimes incite them? Is it surprising that the richer nations are alarmed?

Seemingly we have tended to wait for explosions and then put more money and muscle into trying to subdue them by force than we would have needed in working to prevent them through a peaceful economic solution. In 1968 our military expenditures in Vietnam were about ten times the total nonmilitary assistance budgets in the world. Surely we can focus as much attention, research, inventiveness, and planning on our own programs of economic and technical aid as we now pour into our defense programs.

The Space satellites described in the previous chapter can provide a great share of such aid, if they are used for the benefit of have-not nations as well as for our own enrichment. Many fruitful areas of Earth can provide homes and food for immense numbers of new people, if good plans are laid to attract them there and help them cultivate the land. Even so, it is clear that we must damp the erupting volcano of population. World Bank President Robert S. McNamara has pointed out that a developing country which halves its birthrate can boost its living standards by 40 per cent in one generation. America must help to persuade the underfed and overpopulated nations of the world, in their own interest and ours, that Earth's physical limitations require stabilizing the birthrate. Otherwise an automatic corrective will sooner or later restore the balance: a large-scale "die-off," as biologists call it.

We in the United States often fail to comprehend our real power in the world. It is not military power. It is the power of ideas, of invention, of planning ahead to get necessary jobs done well. We have the know-how and the resources to play a major role in tidying up our cluttered Space Ship Earth, bringing its passenger complement into comfortable balance, making it a place where all people can live healthy lives free from overcrowding and undernourishment. Indeed, we have not only the power but the duty, as individuals, to work toward such ends if we truly believe in the religious concept of stewardship—of proper care and use of resources for the benefit of all. But our capacity for creative leadership will not be usable much longer. We must use it while we can. Each of us can help by asking questions of our elected representatives, by urging action, by alerting others to the corrections that must be made quickly.

6

SOMETHING IN THE AIR

●

There is today a worldwide crisis of the environment. It stems from the extraordinary mass migration from rural to urban areas in all regions of the planet. It stems from a too-rapid increase in population. It stems from helter-skelter urbanization in both the developed and under-developed nations. It stems from abuse and misuse of the Earth's resources. . . . The crisis of the environment is rooted in shortcomings—in failures of design, failures of planning, failures of politics.
—The Overview Group (international consulting firm)

●

It may have been the first prenatal stirrings of the Space Age—the early explorations of the upper air by balloons—that awakened us to a keen interest in the atmosphere surrounding Earth like a protective wrapper. Certainly it was our preliminary probing of Space in the past decade that made us sharply aware that the wrapper may be getting damaged.

The early dreams of eventually leaving Earth had to take account of the atmosphere. In 1865 Jules Verne wrote *From the Earth to the Moon,* in which he visualized a cannon launching a spacecraft. Many of his predictions turned out to be surprisingly accurate, as we know, but no cannon has ever launched a Space vehicle. Why not? One big reason is that the air is thickest and most resistant at ground level, where a cannon expends all its force instantaneously.

Space-dreamers began to comprehend this fact about the air in 1875, when three men made a balloon ascent to a height of six miles. Only one survived. Lack of oxygen killed the others. It was all-too-convincing proof that air was thinner at a little distance from Earth.

So men groped into that vast transparent blanket around the planet. How thick was it? Where did it thin out, and by how much? How did it affect our weather? Why did it become cooler at high altitudes—as mountaineers and balloonists were painfully aware—even when the sun was shining brightly?

Eventually they learned that air was not a simple homogenous substance, as the man in the street supposed. It was a mixture of various gases, and might also sometimes be laden with many tiny floating particles of various solid materials. As for its coldness at great heights, it was too thin up there to absorb much heat; for every three miles of altitude the air density was approximately halved. Above five miles there was barely enough to sustain human breathing. So "outer space" began about six miles up, for unprotected man.

However, rocket experiments in the 1950's showed that even 100 miles up there was still measurable air resistance, caused by molecules of oxygen and nitrogen. Therefore any satellite to be established in a permanent orbit around Earth would have to be still farther up, lest it be gradually slowed by the atmosphere's drag.

In 1960 the United States began sending up "weather-eye" satellites called Tiros, for Television Infrared Observation Satellite. These gave a global view of the blanket that nobody had ever had before. Since then the upper atmosphere has been under intensive study by meteorologists looking for clues to weather prediction; by astronomers seeking to understand other planets by comparing their atmospheres with Earth's; and by Space scientists charting the road into deep Space. Consequently we now know that our atmosphere is neither as simple as it looks from below, nor as shallow as scientists recently supposed. It is many-layered and forever in complicated motion. If some of the layers should alter, all life would perish.

The lowest layer—the few miles down near Earth's surface where life can breathe—is called the troposphere, from the Greek for "sphere of change." Above that is a sandwich of thinner layers called the stratosphere, meaning sphere of layers. This includes layers of the lightest gases such as helium and hydrogen; of certain sulphate particles which may play a role in rainfall; and of ozone—the same clean-smelling blue gas that is often noticeable around ultraviolet lights and electrical generators.

Concentrated ozone would be violently poisonous, so we can be thankful that most of it stays far from us. Enough of it does form sometimes in traffic jams to become an irritant in smog. But up in the stratosphere it performs an amazing protective function. Even though it is a mere wisp of a layer that would be one hundredth of an inch thick at surface pressure, this is enough to soak up ultraviolet rays from the sun which would otherwise kill most forms of life by destroying the vital nucleic acid in their cells. (Since ozone also happens to be a powerful germicide, chemical companies manufacture small quantities of it to sterilize drinking water.)

Men did not learn much about what lay above the stratosphere until they developed telemetering—the technique of "measuring at a distance" by translating the conditions to be measured into electrical impulses radioed back to a receiving station on the ground. Sensors have been developed that can measure almost every conceivable condition—including electric and magnetic fields, light, temperature, motion, pressure, and atomic radiation. The measurements take the form of changes in the intensity or spacing of the electrical pulses. Telemetering is so intricate now that the readings have to be decoded by computers; without it our Space probes would tell us almost nothing.

Rockets and telemetry, then, showed that above the stratosphere there is a warmer layer called the mesosphere, in which millions of meteors from Space are incinerated before they reach Earth. Its warmth is caused by the solar radiation reflected up into it by the ozone below.

About 50 miles above Earth, the mesosphere shades into the weird layer called the ionosphere, a region of flickering auroras and strange electrical activity. There the sun's radiation chips electrons away from the gas atoms and so "ionizes" them, giving them an electric charge. Certain radio waves hitting this layer of charged particles are bent back toward Earth, which reflects them upward again. This is what enables us to communicate long distances around Earth's curvature by radio, despite the fact that radio waves travel only in a straight line. Occasionally the ionosphere also reflects ordinary television signals so they are received thousands of miles away; this happens when storms on the sun intensify the streams of particles and high-energy radiation sent toward Earth, causing the ionized layers to strengthen and thicken. During these sunstorms long-distance radio transmission on Earth is disrupted and sometimes blacked out.

In this chapter we are concerned mainly with what is happening in the lower layers of the atmosphere close to us—because recent studies have shown that we are changing the chemical makeup of those layers. To put it bluntly, for a long time we have been unwittingly poisoning our atmosphere. The most worrisome of the poisons with which we are loading the air is sulfur dioxide.

Sulfur dioxide can combine with moisture to form a menacing sulfuric-acid mist, which can get past the marvelous cleansing devices in the human respiratory tract and burn deep into the lungs. Sulfur dioxide was a chief culprit in at least nine massacres of the past forty years.

Sieges of heavy smog caused widespread deaths in Belgium in 1930; in England three times, in 1931, 1952, and 1956; in Donora, Pennsylvania, in 1948; and in New York City in 1952, 1963, and 1966. In all nine of these mass tragedies, it turned out afterward that nothing extremely unusual had caused them. There had simply been a particularly heavy concentration of the usual poison gases that are already part of the atmosphere in those areas. The trigger was an atmospheric quirk called a temperature inversion, in which a layer of warm air trapped heavily polluted cooler air over the area for several days.

More and more temperature inversions seem likely. The Assistant U.S. Surgeon General predicts, "We're going to have an increasing frequency of episodes in which pollution kills people."

Sulfur dioxide is only one of the harmful ingredients in the awesome 146 million tons of man-made aerial garbage spewed into the United States atmosphere each year. This tonnage outweighs the country's annual steel production! Other leading pollutants in our air include not only the previously mentioned ozone but also carbon monoxide (colorless, odorless, but potentially deadly), benzopyrene (which has given cancer to mice), acrolein (an ingredient in tear gas), peroxyacyl nitrate (a cause of the sore chests, burning eyes and coughing that afflict many people on smoggy days), and countless tiny specks of lead, asbestos, carbon, ash, oil, and grease.

Eighty tons a month of such particles sift onto each square mile of our major cities—putting layers of grime on everything and costing an average city family about $600 per year in washing, cleaning, repairing, and repainting bills. (A cartoon in a magazine shows a lady on the terrace of a modern city apartment building, about to dine outdoors, calling to her husband, "Hurry up, dear, your soup's getting dirty.") If all the grit that drifts onto a typical American city in one year were to tumble to the ground at once we'd be buried in 21 feet of it.

The country's most formidable air polluter is the automobile. At least 90 million automobile tail pipes pour out various contaminants, including tetraethyl lead and carbon monoxide. The lead can slow brain functions and jangle the nerves. The carbon monoxide can lower the blood's ability to carry oxygen. From their vantage point in the purity of Space, our astronauts have seen how big and numerous the ugly brown fogs are. Gemini pilot Pete Conrad shot pictures of some of them to arouse Earthlings. "Notice the air pollution drifting out there nearby," he broadcast, "in case anybody thinks we don't have it."

Dr. Jerome D. Frank of Johns Hopkins Medical School says, "It is estimated that the chances of a man dying between the ages of 50 and 70 from respiratory disease are twice as great if he lives in an air-polluted area rather than in a clean-air area." Emphysema is now the fastest-growing cause of death in the United States. Bronchitis is so common in Great Britain that it is called "the national disease."

Does something in city air cause emphysema, or aggravate it? Why do people who live in the dirtiest air get the most colds, bronchitis, and pulmonary disease? The answers may be as elusive as the air itself. But the search that started with the dawn of the Space Age has lately sent scientists by the hundreds to study air pollution; has led to tests on thousands of animals and humans; has released millions of government dollars through hospitals, universities, research laboratories, and the National Center for Air Pollution Control, a comparatively new division of the U.S. Public Health Service.

Aside from whatever sickness and death it may cause, the horrendous mess that mankind vents into that great sewer in the sky is costly: an estimated $11 billion a year in property damage alone. Polluted air is known to corrode or disintegrate many materials and to damage many growing things. Such diverse plants as orchids and spinach can no longer be grown around Los Angeles. Sulfur dioxide from copper smelting in southeastern Tennessee denuded the landscape of vegetation and poisoned the soil so thoroughly that the area is still virtually bare fifty years later.

Brilliant red sunsets admired in New York and Los Angeles are a danger signal to meteorologists and pollution researchers. They know the red is a warning that the atmosphere is heavily laden with billions of tiny particles in the air, given off by automobiles and industry. What will happen in those angry red skies, the experts wonder, as more and more machines crowd into our fast-growing cities?

When the whole area from Boston to Washington is built up into a megalopolis—one vast city with no open spaces—meteorologists fear that its windbreaks and rising heat will change wind patterns so that no breezes will penetrate into the huge sprawl. People near the center will swelter in what is called a heat island, a phenomenon already mildly perceptible in several cities. Midtown Manhattan at street level is about twelve degrees warmer at night, on the average, than are the Westchester suburbs. In forty years a New Yorker may be able to grow tropical plants on his roof—but the mass of air around him may be so foul that he will scarcely dare step outdoors.

Man also kicks up a great deal of plain ordinary dust whenever a farmer plows a field, a bulldozer levels a tract, a car speeds along a dirty road. Whenever a breeze churns a dust bowl, more dust rises. Glaciers keep a record for us of the amounts of dust in the air, since as ice layers form they trap dust from the atmosphere. A Russian study of this frozen record shows a twentyfold increase in airborne dust since Europe began to industrialize. The increase has been much heavier since 1951. Dustiness is casting a pall over Earth, in the view of Reid A. Bryson, director of climatic research at the University of Wisconsin. "Man is now mucking up the atmosphere to the point where he may be changing the climate of the world," he says. "Increase in dustiness is worldwide."

A dusty world is a shiny world. It reflects more of the sun's energy, so less gets through to warm our planet. Nobody is sure what this means for weather. But Dr. Bryson thinks the thicker dust has brought the northern hemisphere stormier weather in the last century and may be a cause of severe winters and tepid summers in much of the United States and Europe during the past half-dozen years. There have also been more blizzards and hurricanes lately.

On the other hand, some scientists think the past twenty-five years of slightly lower average temperatures are merely a passing squiggle in a thousand-year upward curve into hotter weather. The average temperature in 1890 was 8 per cent cooler than in 1966, they say. The warming could be caused by the steadily growing percentage of carbon dioxide in our atmosphere. Carbon dioxide is harmless enough in itself, but it has a strange effect on climate. Like glass atop a greenhouse, it blocks part of the heat that Earth radiates back into Space. Thus heat accumulates here.

For thousands of years we have sent more carbon dioxide into the sky as we burn more and more "fossil fuels" like coal and oil. The carbon dioxide concentration in the atmosphere has increased markedly since 1890. Some reports say there is 11 per cent more of it, some 14 per cent. In a 1963 study, the Conservation Foundation found the carbon dioxide buildup "not yet alarming," but noted that if it continued, the world's average temperature should rise by about 6.5 degrees. This would change wind and rainfall patterns so completely that California would probably become less habitable than the Sahara, the polar regions would be pleasant, and the glaciers might melt—raising the ocean level enough to drown coastal cities.

Something like this has happened to mankind at least once before. There is scientific evidence that the biblical Flood took place about 4000 B.C. Around that time the sea level rose 45 feet in a few centuries, calculates Rhodes W. Fairbridge of Columbia University.

Carbon dioxide is not a pollutant in the sense of being noxious or annoying. But while a hundred million chimneys are pouring it into the air, our green plants and ocean vegetation are removing less and less (for odd reasons to be seen in Chapter 8). As for downright pollutants, they are still dissolved by a huge natural removal cycle that will protect Earth as long as pollutants do not come too thick or fast. But when and if a saturation point is reached and the removal cycle breaks down, a steady worldwide poisoning of the air will begin, and may be irreversible. We have time to come to grips with the problem, but the time seems to be shortening.

The battle is just starting. When the Public Health Service suggested a minimum level for sulfur dioxide fumes, there were sharp protests from spokesmen of the American Petroleum Institute, the Edison Electric Institute, the National Coal Association, the National Coal Policy Conference, and the United Mine Workers. No legal minimum was set. Most American industries balk at cleaning up their smoke when competitors in other areas go free. And they howl at proposals for a nationwide clampdown. Air conditions differ in every region, they argue, so why lock the same controls on each?

However, the Manufacturing Chemists Association says that 125 of its members now spend $35 million a year to cleanse the many kinds of gas they emit into the air. Industry is also making progress in cleaning up auto exhaust. Give an engineer numbers instead of a vague plea (tell him "cut hydrocarbons to 180 parts per million" instead of "do something about smog") and he may reach the goal or surpass it. Hydrocarbon emissions from new cars have already been cut to a fifth of what they were a decade ago. Carbon monoxide in exhaust fumes is down to less than half of what it was in 1956.

The Industry Emission Control Program, sponsored by Ford and six oil companies, will spend $7 million during 1968-71 to "develop the technology for a reasonably priced gasoline-powered car that will emit virtually no harmful emissions into the atmosphere." Meanwhile William P. Lear, one of the great individual inventors in our history, is at work on a steam-powered automobile that will be pollution-free as well as preferable in comfort, convenience, and economy, he says.

In a 1967 speech, John W. Gardner (then Secretary of Health, Education and Welfare) warned: "We need to look into . . . any means of propulsion that is pollution-free. None of us would wish to sacrifice the convenience of private passenger automobiles, but the day may come when we may have to trade convenience for survival."

By all the portents, mankind's new direction in the next decade will take it into new forms of transportation as well as better air-purifying systems in industry. Of course these particular changes would impend even if there were no Space program. But the Space program has undoubtedly made most of us more aware of the need for them, because of its investigations of Earth's atmosphere —and because it is teaching many people in industry and government to think of Earth as a unit, a self-contained Space ship.

The Space Age has brought us new tools against air polluters. Satellites can monitor pollution areas with sensors able to pinpoint the sources, identify the pollutants themselves, and indicate the direction of their drift. A problem defined is a problem half solved. The problem has been broadly defined as reducing the air's content of sulfur dioxide, dust, hydrocarbons, lead particles, and other dangerous pollutants. There are now plenty of capable problem-solvers in government, science, and industry who recognize this as one of mankind's most urgent problems. But the solutions they find will need the backing of aroused public opinion, public pressure, public action. That is where each of us can help. Today the atmosphere is everybody's business.

7

TROUBLED WATERS

Nothing is more inflammable than water, nothing more vicious than a squabble over riparian rights. On every level of human conduct, from the neighbors disputing a faucet to the State contesting the flow of a river, the sharing of water is alive with dangers.

—James Morris

Without water there can be no life, at least not Earth-style life. It bathes and penetrates every living cell on Earth. Down through the ages man has accepted the water around him as a gift from God—a birthright to be squandered or hoarded as he chose.

Confident of an unending supply from Earth's mighty rivers and regular rains, most of mankind has always wasted water and polluted it. When droughts came, whole tribes migrated thousands of miles in quest of it. Men have fought over water since biblical times at least: Sennacherib of Assyria revenged himself on Babylon by dumping carrion in the city's canals. Today armed

Arabs and Israelis attack each other across the disputed River Jordan.

Anyone viewing Earth as a complex integrated whole—the view that Space travel gives—can see that water is now one of our planet's major problems. We can use spacecraft to help solve the problem, as will appear in a moment.

An observer in earth orbit need not be an expert to perceive that some huge basins and plains are producing little because they lack water. He can see 18,000 miles of Earth's coastlines virtually uninhabited for the same reason, although oceans lap at their shores. He will find farms abandoned in many areas because pumping has exhausted the underground water. Wherever he looks on the globe, he will notice growths of "urban sprawl" that require more and more water for the hordes of newcomers swarming into the human hives.

Man now faces a serious, worldwide shortage of water amid plenty. There are 326 million cubic miles of water on the planet —about 1,100 billion gallons. This would be more than ample for everyone, if it were all fit for use. But 97 per cent of it is in the oceans, too salty for drinking or irrigation. Another 2 per cent is locked in ice caps and glaciers, frozen and unusable. The tiny useful fraction that is left is neither evenly distributed, properly used, nor prudently safeguarded. Even where it is abundant, man is making it unusable by carelessly poisoning it.

Consider, for a moment, the strangeness of water as a substance. Colorless, odorless, tasteless, taken completely for granted in everyday life, it remains the most remarkable liquid in our known universe. Water, for example, is the only substance which commonly exists simultaneously in all three states of matter—as solid, liquid, and gas. But it could not exist as a liquid if our planet were not circling in the narrow belt around the sun where there is neither too much heat nor too little. If we were closer to our heat-giving star, all water would boil into steam. Farther out, it would be permanently frozen. In fact, we judge the possibility of life as we know it on other planets in terms of whether or not their temperatures would permit water to be liquid, and whether they possess water at all. This eliminates most of the planets in our own solar system. Mercury is so hot that lead would melt on it; our enigmatic sister-world Venus seems to be roasting beneath clouds of ice crystals; five others appear to be in such a deep freeze that life is unlikely. Only Mars shows traces of water and is considered as a possible home for simple forms of Earthlike life.

On our own beautiful blue-green planet we can thank water for our mostly moderate climate. Water holds more heat, and cools more slowly, than land masses. The oceans' mighty forces pour energy into the air to drive water-carrying winds and heat-carrying water currents—thus raising low temperatures, lowering high ones. This great heat-transporting engine could not work nearly so well were it not for water's oddest property: it is the only liquid that expands and gets lighter when it freezes. This phenomenon accounts for the fact that ice floats on rivers and lakes and seas, insulating the water below—to the comfort and survival of living creatures there. If water behaved like other liquids, the polar seas would freeze solid, forever blocking the flow of ocean currents and probably plunging many parts of Earth into deathly extremes of cold and heat.

Though limited, Earth's cargo of water is never lessened. In nature's familiar endless cycle, water constantly circulates from the air into the land or sea and back again. Plants transpire (we say "perspire" for people) and thereby add vast quantities of water vapor to the atmosphere. The sea does likewise through evaporation. When the water eventually comes down again as rain or snow or dew, it may soak into the soil to unite with the vast accumulation of ground water under all land. Or it may flow over the surface in streams that converge into rivers rushing to the sea.

Much ground water, of course, is sucked up by roots of vegetation. Man, too, has taken to pumping up ground water through wells. This has thrown various short circuits into Earth's system of water circulation, sometimes with unfortunate results for man.

Some ground water may be trapped in sealed-off pools for long periods of geological time; some may flow to the sea underground without ever surfacing as springs or seepages.

Earth has exactly as much water now as it had before man's time: no more, no less. This is what makes a solution to our chronic water shortages so tantalizing. If only we could use the trillion unavailable gallons!

More than a hundred distillation plants already convert sea water to fresh water. But they are expensive. They deliver fresh water for about $2 per thousand gallons, which adds up to more money than any major community could afford. Most municipal water costs about 25¢ per thousand gallons. On the average, each human being uses 30 per cent more water than he did forty years ago. Since more humans are alive every day, their total consumption is growing awesomely. Many of us will soon be drier and thirstier unless someone finds a cheaper way of getting fresh water from the sea.

Since our "water shortages" are shortages of *usable* water, it is obvious that industry and communities need purification systems that speed our reuse of fresh water supplies. Senator Robert Kerr, who headed a Senate Select Committee on Water Resources, warned in 1961: "Well before the end of the century most Americans will be drinking, cooking with, bathing in, and otherwise using secondhand or thirdhand water."

Only about half of America's municipal sewage systems give any treatment to sewage before flushing it into some river or lake. For example, every day New York City pours 200 million gallons of raw sewage into the Hudson River. The riverbed is now so filthy that scientists estimate the great river would need about fifteen years to cleanse itself even if nothing more were dumped. Governor Rockefeller has described the Hudson this way: "For ten miles south of Albany there are no fish but only sludge worms, leeches, rattail maggots, the larvae of flies—the handwriting on the wall that warns us to stop treating our waterways as if they were open sewers."

Yet the sewage of all municipalities combined equals only half as much as what our industrial plants dump into our waterways. Steel mills empty their pickling vats into handy rivers. Paper mills drop in pulp that rots, using up oxygen. Packing plants disgorge the blood and offal of animals. Dairies discharge whey. Canneries contribute inedible cores, rinds, husks, and pesticide-carrying washings.

Americans who once might be excused for a superior attitude about sanitation after traveling in Asia or the banana republics now come home to find their own rivers, bays, and lakes full of filth which can be smelled if not seen. And they can see that the balance of nature is seriously tilted. Shad and salmon no longer come up many rivers to spawn; huge schools of dead fish have floated to the surface of lakes or been cast up on beaches; certain species of water fowl have virtually disappeared.

The problem is not America's alone. Sullen slimy rivers that once ran silver may be seen in many parts of the world. Most major waterways have become cesspools of progress. France's Seine, which was so clear in the Middle Ages that people on bridges could see the stones and green plants on the bottom, is now a murky gray except for the froth of detergent suds. England's Thames, once a good place to fish for salmon, is devoid of life. Poland's Vistula, from which Warsaw used to draw drinking water, is too dirty to be cleansed by the city's filtration plant.

Industrial mankind is straining the limits of Earth's safety. Unless we stop pollution at the sources, our water bills may go sky-high within the next ten years. Our best chemical methods of converting bad water to good are likely to be almost useless by 1980, experts say, if the flood of pollution keeps mounting at its present rate of increase. In 1965 the Federal Water Pollution Control Administration was set up to prod laggard industries. Its administrator, James M. Quigley, said a year later that industry was reacting to new standards "positively and well." FWPCA's chief enforcement officer, Murray Stein, added: "Industry recognizes it's as good business to have pollution control as it is to have good brakes on automobiles."

Bethlehem Steel has spent $25 million on a complex system to treat waste water in its plant on Lake Michigan. "We have left the conversation stage, and gone into conservation," says the head of Bethlehem's program to control industrial wastes. U.S. Steel recently announced that it had spent more than $235 million since 1951 to clean the air and water in its plants and the oil industry spent almost $75 million in one year on research, control equipment, and facilities to lessen pollution caused by its operations.

Evidently technology is on hand to abate water pollution at the sources. But it is one thing to have the technology and another to generate the determination to foot the bill. Some needed treatment plants are still not being built at all. Representatives of some industries still speak out strongly against any stiffening of pollution laws. Some government officials side with them. A New York State Conservation Commissioner came to the defense of an atomic power plant which had caused an enormous fish kill by its effluent. He described this mishap as "almost in the vein of an act of God." We can assume that he did not really mean to imply that God is dead and has been replaced by a power company. But many big power companies do occasionally seem to consider themselves almost divine. More than a hundred nuclear power plants are on the drawing boards, despite the fact that their hot-water discharges will make other pollutants more poisonous, will make water turbid (preventing adequate penetration by sunlight), will stimulate the growth of noxious blue-green algae (the stink of which can literally peel the paint off nearby houses), and will interfere with the reproductive cycles of fish and other organisms and often kill them outright.

Because of power companies' far-flung expansion plans and their almost unanimous disregard of public protests, state or federal agencies might be expected to insist that all nuclear plants be equipped with cooling devices that would not damage the water. But for the most part this is not the case. The Federal Water Pollution Control Administration cannot act until after a plant has been built and damage inflicted. A bill has been introduced in the Senate by Senator Edward Kennedy, and in the House of Representatives by Congressman Richard Ottinger of New York, calling for a two-year moratorium on nuclear plant construction while studies are made to eliminate hazards. Only widespread public pressure seems likely to push the bill through.

Meanwhile battles are raging against other types of pollution. "Injunction," John E. Teeple once said, "is the most effective spur to progress in chemical industry." Whether this is literally true or not, a few militant conservation groups have been forcing not only chemical companies (which produce 500 or so new compounds each year, many highly toxic and dreadfully persistent in waste water) but other polluters to become more efficient in cleaning up their wastes.

As we saw in earlier chapters, the new instruments for sensing, measuring and photographing can tell us almost anything we need to know about areas below an orbiting space satellite. In the war on pollution they can actually measure the heat of water in streams near large power plants. They can map the distribution of pollutants—and their exact sources—in lakes and bays and the open sea, simply by noting color shades invisible to human eyes. Thus they can quickly detect and identify polluters.

Satellites can also be useful in finding new supplies of fresh water. Ground-water prospecting, as it is called, can be done by satellite to eliminate the need for expensive test wells. The eyes in the skies can "see" accumulations of water trapped underground and tell us where to drill. Eventually, satellites can be the key to enforcement of laws against pollution, but first we must pass the laws. And beyond that we must tax ourselves for better sewer systems, because industrial pollution is only part of the problem, as we have seen. The Public Health Service says we need 50 per cent more municipal sewage treatment plants around the country.

If the public's raw sewage is to be cleaned before it goes into the public's water supply, the nation will have to spend an estimated $600 million per year on the job for ten years. (Another part of the problem, comparatively new but growing fast, is the garbage and sewage dumped from pleasure craft. Seven million boat owners are adding a vast amount of untreated wastes to our waters.)

Is our society aroused enough to cope with these dangers before they become acute? Historically we have been fixers rather than preventers. For generations England talked about the need for underground sewers but did not dig them until polluted water brought on the Black Plague and killed half the population in just two years. In our own time, contaminated drinking water has recently been blamed for outbreaks of typhoid in New Hampshire and hepatitis in Oregon and West Virginia. Isn't this warning enough?

Historians say that people involved in a slowly deepening crisis or upheaval seldom understand what is happening to them. In the fifth century B.C., Athenians realized neither that they were living in a golden age nor that it would rapidly decline. In the last phases of the Byzantine Empire, people were preoccupied with everyday matters while their civilization disintegrated around them.

Our generation is living through the culmination of a struggle between man and nature that began when someone first resolved to bend the forces of nature to his will. Today man is master of the atom and soon the moon. But man's own world is slipping away from him. Too often his habits, his thoughts, his actions, run counter to the basic needs of his existence. He is damaging his planet at a fearsome rate and may soon pass the point where it can sustain human life. Let us hope that enough men realize what is happening, and do enough about it, to prevent irreversible disasters. Each of us can help by seizing every opportunity to urge new respect for nature—especially including water. Though it may be considered a gift of God, water must be harnessed and husbanded by people.

8

NEW SCIENCE TO RESTORE
AN OLD BALANCE

●

We have multiplied inordinately, wasted irreplaceable fuels and minerals and perpetrated incalculable and irreversible ecological harm. I can find no evidence that man contributes anything to the balance of nature—anything at all. On the strength of his knowledge of nature, he sets himself above nature; he presumes to change the natural environment for all the living creatures on this Earth. Do we, who are transients and not overly wise, really believe we have the right to upset the order of nature, an order established by a power higher than man?
　　　　　　　　　—Vice Admiral H. G. Rickover

●

An unfamiliar word is beginning to pop up in public discussions all over America: *ecology*. "Ecology may well become the most popular of sciences—a household word to those masses who today are ignorant of both the word and its meaning," says Prince Bernhard of The Netherlands. "This would not be surprising. . . . The growing realization of the close connection between all that happens on this small planet as a result of men's good will or the lack of it, or of nature's being kind or unkind, will arouse interest in a science that occupies itself with the relationship between the living organism and its surroundings."

This new science studies the cause-and-effect action between various forms of life and their surroundings, and the balance that keeps nature's affairs in order. The word itself was coined a century ago from two Greek words that mean "the study of home." Plants and animals seldom make a mistake in their choice of a natural home. If they do, they die. At any given spot, merely by looking closely at the living things there, an ecologist can tell much about the climate and soil, and even guess the annual rainfall and the depth of the water table. Or, if told the facts about soil, climate, and water in a specific area, he can make some close guesses about the varieties of life there.

Red clover grows only where soil and air contain the right mix of chemicals—and where there are bumblebees, which happen to be the only bees of the right weight and head-size to get inside this clover to cross-pollinate it.

One variety of fiddler crab nests only in sand, another only in mud. One kind of fly makes its home at a hot spring; a spring of no other temperature will do. Even a marsh hawk, which adapts easily and is not finicky about food, lives only in certain kinds of wet woodland.

Animals depend directly or indirectly for their food on green plants loaded with proteins and sugars and starches. Green plants cannot live by themselves either. For eons the green leaf has depended on solar energy to power the greatest factory on Earth. As each tiny particle of the sun's light (called a photon) collides with the leaf, the energy leaps to the leaf's inner machinery, which is the green substance we call chlorophyll. With this energy the chlorophyll smashes open the molecules of water and carbon dioxide that the leaf has taken in through its pores from the air, and silently reassembles them into new structures of basic food.

Meanwhile leaves give mankind the very breath of life. As a leaf converts water and carbon dioxide into food, it pumps out surplus oxygen through its pores in such volume that the air nearby is wonderfully freshened. When car exhausts and factory chimneys spew gases, the oxygen exhaled by leaves helps to purify the polluted air. Without the plants' gentle breathing, all animal life on

Earth would long ago have flickered out like a candle in a shaft full of carbon dioxide.

There is a similar interdependence in the open ocean. There minerals and sunlight nourish the microscopic one-celled organisms called plankton—the "pasturage" devoured by sea creatures of all sizes. Plankton are at the very beginning of the endless chain of who eats whom, but even they rely on the right kind of home. According to their particular species, they flock upward or downward in the sea as the weather changes, seeking the special level where the light intensity, water temperature, and salt content all suit them. If a widespread pollutant such as an oil slick or DDT kills the plankton, all marine life in that area starves or migrates.

Green plants are Earth's most basic resource. Ecologists urge society to think about protecting this resource. Space travel, oddly, has helped society to think in such ways. To leave Earth, man must take a livable environment with him—air, water, and food enclosed in a shell. For the trip to Mars proposed for about 1980, man will need to recycle his wastes and turn them into food—which Earth has always done for him. Familiarity with Space ships is helping him understand Earth, because the ship and the planet are so much alike.

To point up the interdependence of living things, British ecologists like to argue half-jokingly that British sea power was built by old maids. Here is their reasoning: Old maids are well known to love cats as pets. So many English spinsters keep cats that England has few field mice, because cats prey on mice and keep their population down. Field mice eat bumblebee larvae—but where mice are few, bumblebees can swarm. The prevalence of bumblebees in England accounts for the prevalence of red clover, which they alone can pollinate, as we noted a moment ago. Red clover is the chief fodder of British cattle. And bully beef has long been the staple diet of the British navy. Thus it is demonstrated, is it not, that spinsters enabled Britannia to rule the waves?

Less facetiously, it has been shown that many small lakes and bogs in the United States were formed because a Parisian invented the silk hat. When beaver hats went out of style, trappers stopped killing beavers, which made a comeback in America and built many dams in streams.

The point is that Earth is an enormous web of cause and effect. All its soils, waters, climates, and living organisms influence one another. An action in one place produces subtle biological reactions in that place and usually in other places, too. For want of mice, a fox dies. For want of foxes, a lion starves. For want of a lion, all manner of birds and insects, and innumerable other life forms may be thrown into chaos.

The greater the action, the more likely that the ecological reaction will be widespread and often irreversible. This is one of the basic truths about our Earth home, although Western man has largely overlooked it for thousands of years. Sir Francis Bacon, the philosopher-scientist, was one of the few who saw this truth. He warned us three hundred years ago, "Force maketh Nature more violent in return." He also laid down a primary principle of today's ecology, "We cannot command nature except by obeying her."

Long before Christianity, there were pagans who thought that each tree, each spring, each hill had its own guardian spirit. Before they dared to dam a spring or chop a clearing, they prayed to the local spirit in charge and offered continuous sacrifices to keep it appeased. But the whole concept of the sacred grove is alien to Christianity and the West.

While Western man sought to kill or exploit wild creatures, Eastern man continued in awe of them. Millions of Hindus thought it a sin to kill any animal (and still think so, of course). Western man often chuckles at such belief in kinship with nature. As we look at any plant or animal, we tend to ask, "What good is it?" The question comes down from medieval ideas of a small, cozy cosmos in which God had put everything where it was for man's use; from the times before Galileo began to shake our belief in a man-centered solar system; before Newton found laws governing the mechanics of the universe; before Hutton fathomed the immensity of past time; before Darwin put man into perspective with millions of other species evolving on Earth; and before a Vermont scholar, George Perkins Marsh, created the concept of ecology with a fact-crammed, angry book he wrote in 1864: *Man and Nature*, subtitled *Physical Geography as Modified by Human Action*.

Marsh's book, to which we shall return in a moment, attracted little attention when it appeared. His countrymen, true to their heritage from the Middle Ages, continued to consider nature unimportant because it was soulless. If God noticed a sparrow's fall, many devout Christians took this as an example of His omniscience, not of His love. Jesus reportedly gave no thought to the Gadarene swine.

Yet our saintly modern theologian and humanist, Dr. Albert Schweitzer, revered all living things. He wrote: "The great fault of all ethics hitherto has been that they were believed to have to deal only with the relation of man to man." There have been many other Christians with a kindly feeling toward beasts (though not toward most fish, or any insects). St. Francis of Assisi is rightfully their patron and might well be the patron saint of ecologists. It is worth noting that many of his followers were burned as heretics; Francis of Assisi was probably the most radical Christian leader since Jesus Christ.

Even the Eastern civilizations have never felt any great concern for inanimate elements in our Earth home: its forests, soil, air, waters. The idea of deliberately saving part of the wilderness they were conquering has never occurred to pioneers or missionaries in any part of the world. Primeval overgrowth and undergrowth have always seemed enemies to be fought and destroyed, perhaps to be supplanted with bountiful orchards, or with cities and highways. The world seemed so unimaginably huge that nobody could foresee any end to its supply of woodland.

About 1600 B.C. the Shang dynasty began clearing northern China's forests on a vast scale. Thirteen centuries later the Chinese philosopher Mencius saw great herds of goats and cattle (which China cannot support today) grazing and trampling in the last remnants of these forests. Modern China is paying for 3,500 years of ignorant destruction of growth it thought worthless.

India is in a similar plight for a similar reason. Much of the land is only desolate dusty hills. But when Alexander the Great spilled into the Punjab on his way to rule the world, he marched through stately green forests. In later centuries Indian plowmen and their goats and sacred cows destroyed the forests. Unchecked floods followed, ruining the fertility of most of the subcontinent's hills and lowlands.

Until a moment ago, geologically speaking, most land teemed with dense growth. In our mind's eye we can visualize Earth as an orbiting space traveler would have seen it before 10,000 B.C. —league upon league of green for land, blue for the oceans, shining white for the ice caps. Then we can picture the ball changing as man builds empires: the green areas shrink, the waste lands grow. We see the pockmarks of dry lakes, the pustules of strip mines, the scabs that are cities glowing like infections when we circle to the night side. Man seems to have become a disease of nature—perhaps a fatal disease, unless he makes a quick midcourse correction.

To comprehend the scope of that disease, we must scan ancient history as George Marsh did. He noted that in the time of the Roman Emperor Augustus, Adria was a seaport. By the nineteenth century it lay fourteen miles inland. Why? Marsh figured that the Romans had denuded the land, allowing about 220 million cubic yards of soil from the Apennines and Italian Alps to be eroded each year and dumped at the coast. This would cover 360 square miles with seven inches of silt. Marsh found similar blight in almost every country where Rome's legions left "a dying curse to all her wide dominion." Other civilizations have been destructive too, to their ruin. Temple records in Babylon's last decades show steadily shrinking harvests and fewer kinds of fish and game. Plato records that as he and Socrates strolled in Greece's uplands, absorbed in dialogues, they nevertheless could not help noticing how sparse the vegetation was. They knew that past generations had referred to those hills as thickly wooded.

The Crusaders deforested great swaths of Europe and the Middle East to solve problems of supply and transport. Then in the fourteenth century the invention of cannon sent men swarming through forests and mountains for potash, sulphur, iron ore, and charcoal, obliterating much wild life and upsetting biological balances. Closer to home and this century, great cattle drives in the American Southwest turned much of that once-grassy region into dust, too poor to support either livestock or game.

The Soil Conservation Service of the federal government estimates that plows and cattle have now ruined 280 million acres of United States farmland and rangeland—twice the area of France —and have damaged another 100 million acres so badly that they cannot be reclaimed. About one-third of all American topsoil has been blown or washed away. Much of Russia's land will never recover either, ecologists believe, because Khrushchev farmed it so greedily.

Man is a simplifier. The shorter his food chain, the more efficient his conversion of the sun's energy into human food. So he grows huge fields of a plant he can eat or can feed his livestock. All his simplification could ultimately and logically lead to a world without competing forms of life—perhaps man alone, growing his food in vast tanks of algae or chemicals.

But man's simplified food chains are precarious. He must maintain most of his crops and herds by chemicals and machinery, always on guard against infestations of organisms which can multiply fearsomely in a short time. Nature's built-in protection is gone. Man has made wheat and corn dependent on him for their survival; they cannot now procreate by themselves. He has converted the cow from a wild animal, well able to defend itself and its young, into a walking milk factory which would soon fall prey to coyotes if abandoned on the plains.

Man is constantly fighting forms of life he thought he had subdued. To continue growing wheat he must stay one step ahead of wheat rust, breeding new varieties of wheat faster than the fungus can adapt to them. To maintain his orchards he must keep finding new ways to control insects that become immune to his insecticides. His plans for expanding food production always involve large-scale projects to exploit and reshape nature. But now he finds that the more he reshapes nature, the harder it fights back. The more he deforests land, the more dikes and levees and flood-control dams he must build. The more he ignores the needs of wild life, the fewer species there are—and the greater the hazard of unchecked population explosions among others.

Since the birth of Christ, 106 species of mammal have been exterminated, almost a third of them in the last half-century. Another 600 are now threatened by man. There are no replacements. Not one new animal is known to have evolved in the last million years.

While man ponders future chances of colonizing Space, other forms of life are already breeding new colonies on this planet, with unpredictable effects. Wherever there are no natural foes to check them, foreign species are on the march, often unwittingly aided by man, causing drastic changes in natural balances. Armadillos have fanned out from southern Texas into six states. North American muskrats have spread throughout Europe and Asia since the escape of five imported by a Czech in 1905. The Colorado potato beetle, recently arrived in Europe, is causing severe losses. The western deermouse, native of grasslands, is spreading eastward by following the grass shoulders on new highways. Rocky Mountain spotted fever, so named because it afflicted residents of the mountain states, has been breaking out all the way to the Atlantic seaboard; it is caused by a microbe harbored by ticks.

Changes in the communities of living things used to be gradual, over million-year spans, but man has speeded them up. "Make no mistake," says Oxford University's Dr. Charles S. Elton, a world authority on ecology. "We are seeing one of the great historic convulsions in the world's flora and fauna."

Short-range solutions to the pest problem have backfired. A

prime example is our use of chemical insecticides. We began with crude weapons such as arsenate of lead that killed animals and men almost as easily as insects. About 1940 chemists devised the famous chloral compound DDT (dichlorodiphenyltrichloroethane) which killed insects on a vast scale. We did not foresee what other changes it would trigger.

DDT was used in orchards around the world against fruit flies and other insects, such as red mites, which attack fruit. Instead of killing red mites, DDT killed their enemies. Now we have a worldwide nuisance of red mites in orchards. Health authorities in North Borneo decided to fight malaria by spraying villages with DDT. This killed the malaria-carrying mosquitoes, as planned. But more resistant cockroaches absorbed the DDT and survived. The roaches were eaten by larger creatures who in turn were eaten by cats. The DDT killed the cats. Without cats, rats abounded. The health authorities had unknowingly traded the threat of malaria for the threat of plague.

DDT worked well everywhere against the kinds of mosquito that carry the malaria parasite—for a time. But in about a decade a more virulent kind of DDT-resistant mosquito appeared. Moreover, DDT and other chlorinated hydrocarbons are long-persisting poisons that have proved to accumulate in many forms of life, including man. When we dust a field in California to protect a crop against insects, we add to the amount of DDT ingested by snowy owls in the Arctic, penguins in Antarctica, and people everywhere. Virtually everything we eat now contains some DDT.

In 1967 conservationists stocked Lake Michigan with coho salmon fingerlings imported from Oregon. Within a year 20-pounders were numerous and the program was thought to be a spectacular biological success. But in another year hundreds of thousands of young salmon hatched from Lake Michigan coho eggs were dead. Tests showed that DDT was the killer. The Michigan Department of Agriculture had sprayed nearby land to prevent the spread of Japanese beetles into farms. The poison had washed from the land and tainted the lake, just as it has much of the world's fresh water and sea water.

In the water the DDT enters plankton, from which higher forms of marine life absorb it in daily doses that eventually reach dangerous strength. It has been detected, along with various other pesticides, in many species of fish and in the birds that feed on them only to die or stop reproducing. DDT is almost certainly to blame for the alarming scarcity of New England's once-numerous falcons, hawks, and herons—as well as the continent's bluebirds.

In poisoning plankton we are not merely weakening the base of the sea's pyramid of foods. We are changing the proportion of gases in the air. Plankton manufactures 70 per cent of Earth's oxygen by photosynthesis. The vegetation that gives us the other 30 per cent is also being steadily rooted out to make more room for civilization. At the same time we are removing vast quantities of oxygen from the air by burning, and adding carbon monoxide and carbon dioxide. The oxygen content of the oceans seems to have decreased 12 per cent since 1920. Nobody is sure why.

Our species has been destroying forests and other plant life so widely that they may not maintain the age-old balance of oxygen and carbon dioxide. If the current concentration of carbon dioxide in the air should double, that small change would be enough to raise Earth's overall temperature by three degrees. Perhaps such a change is under way. During the International Geophysical Year, 1957-58, investigations seemed to show that the vast glaciers, with their millions of cubic miles of ice, were melting steadily. Some had been retreating as much as 80 feet a year.

The sea level appears to be inching up each year, which could be accounted for by runoff from melting glaciers. At high tide during big storms, the Atlantic now rages almost high enough to begin threatening to flood New York's subways. But the water is not so cold as it once was. Fish that prefer cold waters seem to be migrating northward, while warm-climate trees advance from the tropical zones.

As we scan all these recent changes—disappearance of some species, explosion of others, depletion of the soil and the seas, spread of poisons in water and air and food, ominous quirks in the weather and climate—it begins to appear that men will have to change their ways in order to keep their world habitable. The sheer variety and scale of the things men are doing to the planet suggest that a number of biological balances must be near breaking point.

After ten thousand years of exploiting nature, man finds himself in an industrial world molded closely to what he thought he wanted. But arising from it is some unglimpsed, unintended world, some nightmarish caricature called up like a genie from a bottle. And this genie—nature, an enemy, no longer the kindly Mother Nature of past generations—will seldom obey the men who roused it. It bids fair to become as destructive as a blind Samson. Can we guide it? Can we live in harmony with it? That is the question that lies burning in the bottom of the garbage dumps, in the metal heart of the bulldozers, in the depths of the stinking waters and darkening clouds.

Historically, mankind has been disinclined to worry about distant dangers, disinclined to give up immediate gain for the sake of preventing future disaster, disinclined to work in groups when there is no urgent goal in view. We may be seeing a new onset of the illness that, according to the Spanish philosopher Ortega y Gasset, weakens all civilized societies and eventually kills them— the desire of the citizens to enjoy the fruits of civilization without making the efforts and sacrifices necessary to preserve it. Perhaps the last word was really said by Descartes more than three hundred years ago: "Defects are always more tolerable than the change necessary for their removal."

But let us not throw up our hands prematurely. Certainly there is still a chance to save ourselves. We need only realize—and act on the knowledge—that every man depends on every other man and ultimately on every other creature.

Such knowledge calls for a new type of man—a truly cooperative, brotherly man. Christianity has always exhorted men to love each other, help each other. But now we seem to need an even higher and more vigorous Christianity, with deep concern about what is good and right not only for all mankind, but for the trees and the fish and the living world as a whole. In the words of Aldo Leopold, a great conservationist, we need to develop an ecological conscience.

But what then? Suppose our conscience and hardheaded common sense convince us that we are part of Space Ship Earth and that we must make some sharp midcourse corrections to keep the ship in good working order. How do we proceed? What are the corrections we make?

Do we stop eating animals and vegetables?

Do we give a sickly smile and start uprooting civilization?

Obviously not. We could not, even if everyone's life literally depended on it. But if man, master of the atom and soon the moon, can understand the laws of nature, he can act in better harmony with them. His technology can surely cure most of the troubles it is causing. In using the technology, we will need to broaden our vision and work together for the good of the whole globe. Today our world is too much like an airport with no control tower, or a department store with only departmental managers.

We have flood-control authorities, pest-control authorities, forest authorities, irrigation authorities, highway authorities, airport authorities, public utility authorities, and many others—but few of these have tried to reconcile their own narrow goals with those of others. The result is a chain reaction of conflicting decisions that block any overall look at what we are doing to our surroundings.

In 1969 Senator George McGovern put before Congress a bill that would create a high-level Council of Resource and Conservation Advisers to the President. The council would be made up of three presidentially appointed experts on ecology and natural resources—men with no ties to the great lobbies of industry and the vested bureaucracies. Such a council can take a balanced overall view of what we are doing with the land, air, and water.

The McGovern Bill would also create in Congress two special committees chosen from both houses, made up of members of the four separate committees in each house that now consider resource matters. Such a bill is urgently needed to coordinate the conflicting agencies. It could prevent such competitions as that between the Agriculture Department, which is draining marshes, and the Fish and Wildlife Service, which has been buying new areas and flooding them to provide homes for ducks.

But the bill is opposed by many special-interest groups. It will never pass until the public demands it. An ecological conscience is not yet strong in Congress—nor in many city halls or legislatures. It is up to each of us, as a citizen, to help arouse this conscience everywhere.

Everything depends on improving the quality of our relationships with each other. We may well ask whether mankind will develop understanding, and teamwork, in time to save itself. The right course for each of us would seem to lie in doing all he can to build an informed public interest.

9

WINDOWS ON THE INVISIBLE

●

Among the millions of galaxies, suns, stars, planets and moons, a single human being seems puny.

But the real wonder is this: that Homo sapiens, *with only a pair of eyes, a three-pound brain and a few tools, has penetrated so deeply into this cosmic geography. He has measured distances comprehensible only in millions of light-years; has calculated the weight of giant masses rushing through Space; has determined the chemical composition of heavenly bodies from a tiny beam of light.*
—Ira S. Bowen, Director of Palomar Observatory

●

In the previous five chapters we have seen how the instruments of men have reached out into the atmosphere to bring us a wealth of new facts about it, and have enabled us to see Earth better than any men before us. In this chapter let us take a quick glance at some of the astounding recent discoveries in Space itself.

In the first six years of the Spage Age astronomers learned, beyond theory or doubt, that what had seemed empty is teeming with vast interacting forces and energies, stretching down from the farthest galaxies to Earth, and with matter, sometimes in strange forms neither gassy nor liquid nor solid.

Our first Space probes found a great invisible halo of radiation around the Earth, starting above the ionsphere about 1,000 miles out and extending to about 40,000 miles. The halo is made of electrically charged particles from the sun and from Space, trapped by the Earth's magnetism until they spiral far enough out to escape from it. This is the magnetosphere, the last boundary between our planet and interplanetary Space.

The magnetosphere is constantly buffeted by a mighty stream of particles from the sun—the "solar wind." This stream compresses the halo on the sunlit side of Earth and blows it out on the dark side, perhaps 100,000 miles or more. The solar wind seems to be a colossal, continuous explosion; every second the sun blasts out a million tons of matter in every direction. This is the force that keeps the ion tails of comets pointed away from the sun, regardless of whether the comet is moving toward the sun or away from it.

Fierce solar flares, magnetic storms, and other awesome cosmic phenomena erupt from the sun's seething surface and trouble all the gulfs between the planets. Huge clouds of plasma (electrically charged gas which acts more like a fluid in some ways and really is a distinctively different form of matter) periodically churn the solar wind into tremendous magnetic storms, producing fluctuations in Earth's magnetic field that make compass needles waver crazily and sometimes drain power from our long-distance electrical lines to trigger automatic shutdown mechanisms.

Solar activity can also disrupt radio communications, since the ionosphere, the electrified layer of our atmosphere that bounces long-distance radio waves around the curve of Earth, becomes choppy when plasma penetrates it. Broadcasts are weakened or garbled for periods lasting from minutes to several hours; teletypes print gibberish. Therefore one of the urgent goals of today's astronomy is to learn to predict stormy weather on the sun. With a few hours' warning of a solar flare, radio men can figure out in advance which frequencies will be guided most dependably by the ionosphere during the storm, or else can cut down on transmission to insure that high-priority messages get through.

Among the scientists now studying the sun's violence are members of a new, specialized profession: solar meteorology. Using the Essa-type satellites mentioned in Chapter 4, they soon may be able to predict the onset of major turbulence in the sun. This will be important for the protection of astronauts as manned Space flight becomes more common. Anyone who happened to fly through a solar flare (which suddenly licks out millions of miles, with the force of a billion hydrogen bombs) would be destroyed.

Up to 1960, knowledge of the universe seemed well settled. A few loose ends and puzzles persisted, but generations of study through telescopes had—we thought—mapped most major features of the cosmos. There were our neighboring stars, ranked from blue and red giants down to white dwarfs—all suns, all great thermonuclear furnaces, burning hydrogen into helium and then into all the elements. If we think of our sun as the size of a period at the end of this sentence, the sun closest to it is another dot ten miles away. The 7,000 stars seen by our naked eyes, plus tens of thousands of others visible only to telescopes, are all part of one tremendous conglomeration or galaxy, the Milky Way, numbering about a hundred billion stars, turning slowly in a disc so huge that light takes eighty thousand years to cross it. (Each light-year is a stride of six trillion miles.)

In this galaxy, our sun was known to be only a middle-size yellow dwarf somewhere near the rim, taking a quarter-billion years to go round the hub despite its tremendous speed of more than 13,000 miles per second. Beyond lay more than a billion other galaxies in the range of man's telescopes. The closest galaxy to ours—the Magellan Clouds—is so far away that if we shrank the universe to a scale model in which our Earth and sun were separated by half an inch, we would have to put the Magellan Clouds about a million miles away. Some galaxies look much older than others, but nobody is sure why. And all these galaxies strangely seem to be rushing away from one another at unimaginable speeds in an eternally expanding universe, like a colossal puff of smoke.

Long ago astronomers learned to measure distances and speeds by peculiarities of light. In 1800 an astronomer observing the sun began experimenting with various combinations of colored glass. He was startled to notice that certain combinations stopped most of the sun's light but none of its heat, while others blocked the heat but let the light through. This shattered the long-accepted idea that sunlight and heat were the same and therefore inseparable.

The astronomer William Herschel next tried another simple but interesting experiment. He spread a beam of sunlight into a rainbow with a prism, and held a thermometer in the various color bands. He found that temperatures were hotter at the red end of the spectrum than at the violet end. Most surprising of all, temperatures got higher yet beyond the red, where nothing could be seen!

Something quite independent of visible sunlight must be generating this heat. The invisible sunbeams Herschel had discovered became known as infrared—below the red. We now know that more than half the sun's radiation is in the infrared. And we know that we too can create infrared rays merely by striking a match.

A German physicist, exploring the violet end of the spectrum, discovered another kind of invisible radiation beyond that border. This ultraviolet light, as it was called, led us to the realization that visible light makes up only a tiny fraction of the whole spectrum. The "light" spectrum began to expand at both ends. Above the brightest visible blues in the spectrum are not only ultraviolet waves but Xrays and then gamma rays of an infinitesimal trillionth-of-an-inch wave length. (Gamma rays, an undesirable emission of nuclear bombs, are used in the Geiger counters that guide uranium prospectors.) Below the darkest visible red light are the infrareds and then the microwaves, radio waves and—newly discovered—"micropulsations" that reach wave lengths of millions of miles.

Thus the light spectrum has broadened enormously into what is called the electromagnetic spectrum because its radiations are both electrical and magnetic. It embraces an immense family of waves about sixty times the size of the original visible spectrum. The secrets of the universe may be written largely in waves.

Life could not have evolved on Earth had the surface not been blanketed by the atmosphere against invisible bombardments of ions and electrons from Space. However, the atmosphere has been a chronic nuisance to astronomers. Even when clear to the naked eye, it crawls and shimmers with turbulence, like the air above a hot pavement, and distorts the light that gets through. It makes viewing the grandeur of Space the equivalent of studying the world from the bottom of a deep pool of water.

Until recently men had only a small window to peer through— the narrow band of visible light. Then, while a radio engineer studied the static that afflicts radio reecption, he noticed some pulsing noises he could not trace to man-made sources. He finally found that this static was caused by radio waves emitted from distant stars. Thus man got another slot through which to study Space—radio astronomy, of which more in a moment. It is one of the towering feats of the human mind that through these two narrow slits we have pieced together so coherent a view of the cosmos.

For the past century, spectroscopes have been used in every major observatory to fan out the peacock tails of starlight. A spectroscope's prisms or gratings take apart the white radiance from a star into a series of colored bands corresponding to all the wave lengths of light. When this spectrum is photographed, bright or dark lines show up at certain wave lengths, arising from the main chemical elements at the source of the light. Any element, glowing in the furnace heat of a star, emits light at specific wave lengths. The colorful pattern is different for each element, as unique and characteristic as fingerprints. By comparing the lines in a star's spectrum with those on a standard laboratory spectrum, an astronomer can identify the atoms pulsating billions of miles away. Thereby he knows what the star is made of, just as accurately as if he had a sample. So much for the influential thinker August Comte, who remarked in 1840 that mankind must forever remain ignorant of the composition of the stars. Ten years later the spectroscope proved him wrong.

The spectral lines reveal other information too: the speed of a star moving toward or away from the solar system.

Computing a star's distance and motion is done by using a tricky but long-known phenomenon. When an object moves toward us, all its waves of light or other radiation are physically shortened—that is, the crests of the waves are closer together than usual as they reach us, just as the bow of a moving boat piles up waves ahead of it. Conversely, when an object moves away, each wave (of light or sound or whatever) takes slightly longer to reach us. In each case the size of the shift in wave length tells how fast the body is approaching or moving away. A familiar example is the whistle of a passing locomotive, which rises to a scream as it approaches, then drops to a moan, or lower frequency, as it recedes.

In the case of a star, if it is traveling toward us, more light waves are crowded into each second, so the light we see is shifted toward the high-frequency violet end of the spectrum. But if the star is moving away, fewer waves arrive per second and the light shifts toward the low-frequency red end of the spectrum.

As far back as 1912, astronomers began to notice that all galaxies outside our own gave off reddened, shifted light. They also were amazed to find that the farther they looked out, the farther the spectral lines of the galaxies were shifted toward the red end of the spectrum. The greater the red shift, the faster the galaxy was presumably rushing outward, and the farther from us it was. Observers were forced to the conclusion that the entire visible universe—hundreds of millions of galaxies—was not stable, but was expanding in every direction like a balloon, so that all galaxies were fleeing from us and from one another, at speeds up to about 90,000 miles a second for the farthest known galaxies. This is half the speed of light. Astronomers think that when we look at the galaxies we are seeing them as they were a billion years ago or more.

All sorts of ideas were tested on the famous phenomenon of the red shift, as scientists tried to explain away the outflying of the galaxies. But so far the only explanation of red shift widely accepted is that it really depicts a universe that is rushing outward in all directions.

In the meantime, a new kind of eye had been developed for peering farther into the depths of Space. The fact that stars broadcast noise was discovered in 1931 almost by accident, as mentioned earlier. But astronomers were slow to realize that such radio energy—the only radiation besides visible light that can penetrate Earth's atmosphere over a wide frequency range—might offer a new way of "seeing" the invisible.

The discovery seemed interesting but impractical. The radio waves from Space were very short, and devices for detecting feeble beams of such radiation had not yet been developed. However, in World War II the effort to make radar practical had evolved new abilities to detect just such radiation. Moreover, while developing radar, British scientists found that the sun interfered with their efforts by sending out continuous static in the microwave bands. This aroused their interest. They pioneered in building huge dish-shaped antennae to collect signals from Space. Their 250-foot dish at Jodrell Bank was the first big radio telescope.

Radio telescopes had a much longer range than optical telescopes. But at first they could not pinpoint the sources of signals they received. The trouble was that even short radio waves are at least a thousand times longer than ordinary light waves; and the longer the waves, the more blurred the reception. Trying to spot the exact source or distance of faint radio beams was like trying to find distant street lights seen through a fog. All that came through was a vague smear of radiation.

So a great effort got under way to sharpen radio accuracy. If a signal is received simultaneously by two separate radio telescopes and the two signals are combined in one receiver, they alternately strengthen and dim each other, creating what is called an interference pattern. Since the intensity of the pattern is sharpest when both instruments are pointing precisely at the source, they can plot its location fairly closely. The most ambitious scheme for utilizing this principle was undertaken by California Institute of Technology, in cooperation with a team of Swedish astronomers.

They set up one radio dish in California's Owens Valley, and another in Sweden. The two are synchronized by atomic clocks so that they focus simultaneously—or within a millionth of a second—on the same celestial object. According to Marshall Cohen of Cal Tech, this gives a focus at least 500 times sharper than anything astronomers can bring in with the 200-inch telescope on Mount Palomar. "It's like being able to focus a Mount Wilson telescope on a postage stamp in New York," he said at a press conference in 1968. An optical telescope, to do as well, would need a mirror four thousand miles wide.

Meanwhile astronomers from Cornell University went to Arecibo in Puerto Rico and built a gigantic steel-mesh dish reflector that covers 18½ acres, cradled in a mountain bowl. Stood on end, this disc would loom over almost every skyscraper in New York. It is not so accurate as the California-Sweden tandem, but can pick up weaker radio waves from farther out in Space—noise as faint as one thousandth of a millionth of a watt. In its control room, humming and blinking computers calculate the angle from which a radio beam arrives, and then guide the receiver into position to tune in closely. In this way the telescope can "see" twelve billion light-years away—three times farther than optical telescopes.

All over the world, astronomers have been building steel-ribbed parabolic dishes and ungainly rows of spindly antenna arrays, and have begun gathering the celestial sizzling and squeaking that make up the radio music of the spheres. For the fun of it, radio astronomers sometimes connect amplifiers and loud speakers to their antennae so they can hear the Space broadcasts as audible sound. They say that the Milky Way hisses continuously, the sun sighs from time to time, and the planet Jupiter gives deep angry growls like the old Roman god of thunder himself.

Of course astronomers do not expect to learn anything by listening to the celestial chorus. They learn by machine analysis of the radio emanations. To filter out unwanted signals, they feed the impulses from their antennae into amplifiers, and thence into computers for sorting out Space noises from Earthly static. The radio telescope does not form an image of anything at which it is pointed. It can only record the intensity (loudness) and direction of radio waves.

Its value lies in the fact that radio waves sift through many regions of Space where light waves are blocked. These waves, translated into a wiggly line on a moving strip of paper, tell astronomers about parts of the universe that either shed no light or are hidden from view by heavy concentrations of gas, dust, stars, and other peculiar shapes still unidentified.

When a groping radio telescope points directly at a source of radio energy, a large peak appears among the squiggles on the paper. The mere existence of the radio-signal peak proves that something is out there—a fact that often cannot be established in any other way. Its wave length may hint at what the something is; a shift in wave length gives the speed and direction of the broadcaster's motion. Also, the height of the peak can be used to calculate the temperature of the object. Thus radio telescopes are trillion-mile thermometers. By marking the strength and direction of the radio hot spots on sky maps, they have gradually sketched a picture of the heavens quite different from the picture seen by optical telescopes. So we know that ours is at least a dual universe. Some things we see and feel, some we don't.

In two decades the computerized ears of radio telescopes have heard the monstrous churnings of many bodies that are hidden from ordinary light-gathering telescopes: gigantic unlit ten-million-mile clouds of hydrogen gas floating between stars; runaway galaxies; colliding galaxies; and exploding stars (supernovae). In the past seven years they have located things that defied explanation.

Early in 1963, radio astronomers picked up mysterious radio waves so torrential that they must come from something radiating with the power of fifty large galaxies. When skeptical observatories turned their great glass eyes on the areas from whence these signals came, they saw the sources. They were not new discoveries at all. They had been catalogued as dim, puny stars thought to be nearby in our own Milky Way.

But if they were giving off such fierce radio waves, then they could not be stars at all, because no stars—only whole galaxies—radiated powerfully enough to be heard here. Apparently they were bigger than a star but smaller (yet much, much brighter) than a galaxy. For want of a better term, these peculiar beacons came to be called quasi-stellar (starlike) radio sources, a name soon contracted to quasars. Spectroscopes analyzed quasars' light. It was baffling. The few lines visible were in locations that did not jube with any known element. Nothing like these spectra had ever been observed before.

Studying them with electronic gadgets sensitive to invisible infrared, astronomers found that the lines fell into place, matching known elements, if the spectra were shifted far back along the comparison scale into the infrared. The "red shift" mentioned a few pages ago was present, but it went clear off any previously known scale. If the red shift meant the same thing throughout the universe, these objects must be moving faster than seemed possible—and must be farther away than anything else ever seen. Their distances were computed at six to ten billion light-years. At one glance, so to speak, man had suddenly doubled his horizon. As one leading astronomer phrased it, the world of science "went into a state of complete shock." As far as anyone can tell yet, the quasers are utterly impossible. Either our most painstaking observations are all wrong or the quasars follow laws wholly unknown.

To appear as bright as they do at such immense distances, these objects must glow with the brilliance of dozens of galaxies. Yet if they contained anything like a hundred times as many suns as are in the Milky Way, their girth should be so huge that they would show up as tiny cloudy patches, even at their enormous distances. From their pointlike appearance, it seems they must be small—not more than ten light-years across. Some ninety quasars have now been found, all of apparently unthinkable distances.

With a size only a fraction of a galaxy, the quasars are each pushing out up to a hundred times more light than an entire galaxy of stars. How to explain this incredible output of energy is a problem heating up many a scientific meeting. "Are we looking at an elephant a mile away, or a mouse two feet away?" asked George Gamow, a noted physicist.

Can there be something about quasars that makes the enormous red shift of their light mean something quite different from what it means elsewhere? The law of the red shift, accepted as the astronomical measuring stick of speed, has suddenly become suspect. Perhaps the speed of light, the one great constant of the universe, is inconstant after all.

Looking into the enormous abyss of time at these long-ago, fast-moving conflagrations, a nonastronomer may wonder for a moment if we should hurry to study the quasars and the galaxies before they vanish forever out of range of all our instruments. But even at such awesome speeds as eight-tenths the speed of light, which some of them seem to have attained, they are not getting perceptibly farther away from us when we consider the colossal scale of the universe. If a person stands in New York and takes one step east, we would not consider him significantly farther away from Los Angeles. But, relatively speaking, he would have receded much more perceptibly than a quasar will recede from Earth in a century.

Other objects besides the quasars have defied explanation lately. In 1965 a whole new class of distant objects came into view, bodies that were ablaze with ultraviolet light but emitted no strong radio signals. These queer, brilliantly blue "interlopers" or "peculiars," as astronomers dubbed them, now seem to be just as far away as quasars but much more plentiful. The quiet blue galaxies or blue quasars will be another rich field of puzzlement for astronomers.

But more puzzling of all, so far, are some regularly beeping radio pulsations, coming weakly but with such fantastically precise regularity that scientists fleetingly wondered if some intelligent beings out there were trying to communicate. The notion was soon dropped, although a few scientists are still wondering.

The ghostly beeps were first received early in 1968. Since then they have been heard again and again, sometimes louder and sometimes fainter, but always coming from the same place in the sky, showing that the source lies beyond our solar system. By the end of 1968 some two dozen pulsing radio sources, nicknamed pulsars, had been located by radio observatories. Early studies indicated that pulsars would have to be dense, compact bodies— smaller than Earth, yet heavier than the sun.

Only two kinds of stars answered this description. One of them has long been known as a white dwarf—a strange star formed in the blink of an eye, astronomers think, by the burning-out of its hydrogen fuel. Our own sun is expected to reach this dying throe about six billion years from now. As the star's core stops burning, gravity pulls the shell inward and crushes all the atoms, so that the dull-glowing matter is packed together with almost no waste space. A handful of material from a white dwarf would weigh several tons.

These shrunken suns are plentiful in our galaxy. But their faintness means we can see only the closer specimens. Why should these pulse so regularly?

Perhaps the pulsars are not white dwarfs but neutrons. A neutron star has never been seen. It is purely theoretical, believed to be what results when a giant superstar grows old: it explodes and the residue at its fiery heart collapses under the weight of its own gravity, shrinking so much that the inward pressure jams electrons and protons together to form a hard mass of uncharged particles called neutrons. The mass would be so incredibly dense as to require a new set of physical laws to deal with it.

A neutron star, if it really exists, may be only a few miles across. It would probably spin at a fantastic rate of several hundred revolutions per minute. A matchbox of material from a neutron would weigh not just tons, but billions of tons. Its extremely hot mass would generate such powerful magnetism (billions of times stronger than Earth's) that plasma clouds adrift in Space would be sucked toward it and forced to spin along with it. Though a neutron star may be so tiny as to be lost in the vastness of its plasma cloud, the atoms and electrons on the outer edge of the whirling cloud should be zipping in their great arc at almost the speed of light, emitting energy like the flashes of light from a lighthouse.

Stars spinning and vibrating in their death throes might emit such coughs of static as are reaching Earth. And of course they would be too small to be seen through terrestrial telescopes. But in 1969 astronomers at the University of Arizona spotted a visible star exactly where radio telescopes had placed a pulsar, and flashing at a rate identical to the pulsar's beeps. Pulsars are now being picked out by giant radio telescopes and other instruments at the rate of about five a month. The nearest is estimated to be at least a thousand light-years from us. This indicates such a massive source of power that a totally new equation of physics may be needed to explain it. Moreover, the latest evidence indicates that the pulsars are indeed neutron stars: dramatic confirmation of a bold old astronomical theory.

And what of Unidentified Flying Objects—the controversial and (most scientists confidently insist) imaginary flying saucers? Could the beeps come from such craft? Can astronomy's new instruments find any sure sign of life in the vastness around us?

So far the answers are no. Pulsars do not move across the skies. They are therefore receding from us across gulfs that no living creatures could cross, even at light's speed, in billions of years.

If another world is watching us—say from a base on one of the thirty seldom-seen moons of this planetary system, or from a planet of a nearby sun in our galaxy—its couriers must travel in ships that violate the laws of physics as we know them today. This is not to say that such travel is altogether impossible. Somewhere there must be civilizations much older than ours. Our own brief culture has been evolving for only a millionth of Earth's probable past history. Just as any day-old infant must be younger than most living people, our civilization must be much younger than some others. How can we be sure what is possible for some race vastly older than our own? If our technologies keep on progressing as fast for the next 100,000 years as they have progressed during the 140 years since Michael Faraday made the discovery that led us to the use of electricity, who is to say that we can never send flying saucers to other worlds?

At least one astronomer feels hopeful. J. Allen Hynek, director of Northwestern University's observatory and the Air Force's long-time consultant on flying saucers, writes:

> There is a tendency in the 20th century to forget that there will be a 21st century science, and indeed a 30th century science, from which vantage points our knowledge of the universe may appear quite different. We suffer, perhaps, from temporal provincialism, a form of arrogance that has always irritated posterity.

Astronomers assure us that no form of life can possibly exist on other bodies in our own solar system. A century ago, biologists were equally sure that no life could exist in the depths of our oceans.

Pulsars, blue quasars, radio quasars, and other strange radiations from eons ago are more interesting to astronomers than hypothetical UFO's. Just as tantalizing are the flamelike outbursts of energy from them—energy mostly in the form of radio waves, rather than light or heat; energy so prodigious that no nuclear fission known on Earth or in the sun could produce it. Just as thermonuclear energy was first discovered in the stars, so the study of these faraway bodies may eventually show us entirely new and much more gigantic forms of energy—even, perhaps, new principles for generating power and for converting, combining, multiplying, and transmitting it. If physicists ever fathom the mechanics of these elemental reactions far out at the boundaries of perception, they may yet learn the ultimate secrets of matter and energy on Earth.

Scientists have been duly grately for their two peepholes on the universe, but they are not satisfied, for these two slits are narrow indeed. Light waves and radio waves are only small segments of the enormously wide spectrum of waves. It includes everything from tiny gamma rays, less than a billionth of a micron long, to mile-long radio waves. So the professional star-gazers have long yearned to get out into the full grandeur of Space, to map the universe in all its many "lights."

In 1945 rockets began to poke their noses briefly above the atmosphere, carrying telescopes and spectrographs to snatch some data before falling back. With the dawn of the Space Age in 1957, sounding rockets soared higher and brought in tantalizing hints of greater discoveries to come. They indicated, for instance, that hot stars seem to be pouring out much less ultraviolet radiation than our theories predicted they should. If so, the stars burn hydrogen more slowly than was thought, and the whole timetable of stellar evolution may have to be lengthened.

Another find by the rockets was a huge beam of Xrays, undetectable from Earth, about a thousand times more intense than those from the sun or any known stellar sources. It comes from the approximate center of our galaxy. No one is sure what could be generating such fierce rays. It could be a cloud of hot gas, an invisibly exploding star, or some still-unguessed kind of celestial body fairly near us. Lately a dozen more Xray sources have been found, all within the Milky Way. The strongest is sending rays that must be trillions of times stronger than the sun's.

Gamma rays from unknown sources are likewise plentiful in certain areas, according to the rockets' readings. To explain such a sizzling flux of Xrays and gamma rays, the new rocket astronomers are as puzzled as the radio men studying pulsars and quasars. More sensitive instruments of longer range are needed to fix the sources more exactly.

The instruments are coming, a whole new array of them. In 1962 our satellites in Space began to thrust telescopes through the atmospheric veil and give us longer looks at the star-blaze of infinity. In the previous fifteen years scientists had accumulated only three hours of ultraviolet sungazing and stargazing with rockets, but with the advent of the unmanned Orbiting Solar Observatories instruments were pointed steadily at the sun for thousands of hours, telemetering back mountains of information that is still being digested.

And with the Orbiting Astronomical Observatories, each probing the heavens with eleven different kinds of instruments, we are beginning to see the unknown universe of ultraviolet stars and nebulae. At infrared wave lengths we may be able to glimpse the birth of stars inside opaque clouds of dust and gas, just as a photographer uses an infrared filter to penetrate haze. At radio wave lengths that cannot be detected by ground-based receivers, we may hear news of stellar growth and evolution. All these nonoptical radiations originating in Space offer the scientist unique clues to fundamental processes of the universe.

And so while the astronauts physically broke the bonds of Earth, the astronomers have mentally pushed back the limits of the universe and torn down walls that blocked our view. At the tip of their instruments' present reach, the long-ago birth pangs of the universe may still be recorded in eternally flying waves of radiation. But a programmed instrument may take many years of scanning to find the facts we seek.

The next step in astronomy lies in manned orbiting observatories, so that scientists need not sift endless reports from robots but can swing their instruments to follow anything interesting that they glimpse. Until then we are teased by clues that indicate how enigmatic the universe remains in the face of our ingenious efforts to understand it. When we have a really big observatory in Space, or better yet on the moon, our progress of recent years will seem no more than a prelude to the grandeur that will then open before us.

10

WHY GO TO THE MOON?

●

"What's the point? Who wants to go out into Space
while there's so much to be done here on Earth? There's
not a single planet in the solar system where men can live.
The moon is a burnt-out slag heap, and everywhere else
is even worse. This is where we were meant to live."

"How do you know where we were meant to live? After
all, we were in the sea for about a billion years before we
decided to tackle the land. Now we're making the next
big jump. I don't know where it will lead—nor did the
first fish when it crawled up on the beach."
  —Arthur C. Clarke in *The Other Side of the Moon*

●

There is no single compelling reason for putting men on the
moon. There are dozens of good technical and economical reasons.
Together they make an almost overwhelming case, but few people
—even scientists, who mostly stick to narrow specialties—have
looked at many of these reasons. Let us consider some of them.

One reason for the whole moon program is to create an interplanetary transportation system, with the moon as a goal that
just happens to be available. There is nothing nearer in Space than
the moon. Mars or Venus could have been picked, but were too
difficult as a first step.

Lindbergh, who was a one-man Space program in his day, chose

Paris as the goal for his pioneering flight across the Atlantic—with much the same motives that led President Kennedy and NASA to choose the moon. Lindbergh could have gone by boat if he just wanted to be in Paris. He could have picked Dublin if his only wish was to fly the Atlantic. He could have hovered over America if he merely meant to prove that an airplane could stay in the air a long time.

Lindbergh picked Paris because it was a dramatic goal, and was about as accessible as any European city. But his real goal was to prove that aviation had made Atlantic flights feasible. If the Apollo flight to the moon was a stunt, so was Lindbergh's flight in 1927. But it helped convince mankind that air travel was a reality; and it helped launch the new science of aeronautics (which had been creeping slowly ahead since 1903) on an era of galloping advances. Within forty years, twenty thousand people were flying the Atlantic every day!

The real goal of the Apollo program is to prove that the Space Age now makes it possible for men to explore other celestial bodies. As Brainerd Holmes of NASA said at the outset, "The lunar program makes sense only if we go on from there."

Long after the moon landings are a footnote in history, Apollo will be remembered as the means by which mankind hoisted itself from its Earthly cradle and began to wander about in the cosmic neighborhood. As an interplanetary transport system, Apollo opens the moon and the solar system to human exploration. NASA's head during its years of preparation for the Apollo missions, James E. Webb, said in a lecture at Harvard,

> The Space capabilities demonstrated in 1967 represent—or can be parlayed into—better than 90% of everything we would need to carry out almost any mission that even the most daring have placed on our Space agenda for the next decade.

> The Saturn V-Apollo system permtis us to operate as far out as the moon with payloads of 100,000 pounds. This distance requires about 98% of the energy it would take to operate out to any other place in the solar system.

And it enables us to use all the maneuvers needed anywhere in Space—launch from Earth, orbit around Earth, propulsion and guidance to reach another body, ability to slow down and go into orbit around another body, to land a payload on the surface of that body, and to return to Earth either a part of the payload or the scientific measurements obtained.

Space experts have tried for years to impress this idea on the public. After his circumnavigation of the moon, astronaut Jim Lovell wrote: "The moon is a convenient body on which to prove out our systems and programs. It will always be, for Space travelers, a handy way station."

In the moon's vacuum, where there is no air friction and the gravity is only one-sixth that of Earth, we can launch spacecraft more easily and cheaply than we do here. So it will be not only a test tube for Space systems but a springboard into Space.

It can also be the site of the most useful observatories yet conceived. It is an astronomical satellite already in orbit, with a firm base awaiting only our telescope and observer. The moon has just enough gravity to enable us easily to erect mammoth telescopes, radar and radio facilities, supported with only the flimsiest structures. A telescope on the moon, free from the wavering haze of Earth, may tell us more about the universe in one year than Earthbound astronomers have learned in all previous history. And the moon's advantages for radio astronomy are especially enticing: the far side of the moon is the one place in the entire solar system where radio telescopes would never be made useless by electrical interference from television stations, thunderstorms, and electric shavers. Two thousand miles of solid rock permanently shield the back of the moon from our noisy planet. The low gravity and absence of wind will permit radio telescopes to be built there with parabolic dishes hundreds of miles wide, to "see" what lies beyond the shining island of the farthest galaxies yet known.   •

Another reason for putting men on the moon is that some years hence, when we have established a good-sized Luna City, its industrial plant can manufacture materials and goods never made on Earth. The vacuum and low gravity of the moon, its very low and very high temperatures, are free. Vacuum is a remarkably good insulator, as anyone knows who has used a thermos bottle, yet a big enough vacuum chamber to meet some needs of modern industry is fabulously expensive if it can be engineered at all; on the moon workmen would have access to one merely by stepping outdoors. Similarly, joining some of the newer, tougher metals is next to impossible here—but on the moon, most of them need only be touched together to make a perfect weld. Such advantages will enable manufacturers to build new characteristics into products.

For similar reasons Luna City's laboratories can house a fantastic array of experiments in biology, zoology, medicine, and physics. All our electronics wizardry, for example, depends on vacuum technology, so an unlimited vacuum may lead to unimaginable new inventions. Experiments now requiring days could be tried in minutes.

Likewise, we know that all Earthly organisms are shaped by their lifelong struggle against Earth's gravity. What will happen when they are featherlight? And what will happen when scientists can manipulate algae and microbes under lunar conditions? Will an explosion of growth produce giants? As for metallurgists and chemists, what totally different substances will solar furnaces, ultracentrifuges, and other exotic lunar facilities enable them to create? Nobody knows what our moon colony may produce until it is there; this is one of the best arguments for its existence.

Of course we will not be able to build Luna City so long as most construction materials have to be shipped from Earth. So one of the first jobs will be to use the moon's natural resources. These may be assets worth more to Earthmen than diamond fields or cattle. For all its bleakness, the moon holds a large store of oxygen locked chemically into its basalt rock. It holds silicon for glass, for cement and microelectronic devices. It holds sulfur, iron, cobalt, and nickel. It holds at least traces of magnesium, aluminum, chromium, copper, phosphorus, carbon, sodium, potassium, calcium, and titanium. How can we be sure that all these elements are on the moon? Because even if they are not in the moon's own native ores or compounds, they are known to be in the big and little chunks of the universe we call meteorites, peppered all over the moon's surface. It may also contain strange, unstable chemical compounds that could not exist for an instant on Earth but are kept intact on the moon by vacuum and cold.

The first iron industry on Earth used meteoritic iron. The first industry on the moon will doubtless do the same. There will be plenty of water—because whatever the moon is made of, we can use it to make water and oxygen, if necessary. Industry has already proved out the processes. Studies have also indicated we can set up a small nuclear-fueled power plant to generate electricity. So we already have virtually all the tools and know-how we need to establish a permanent manned base on the moon, then to enlarge it year by year (with perhaps two Saturn-Apollo flights per year) until we have a good-sized city. Most of what we will need can be manufactured there.

But before we dig the foundations we must learn a lot more about the moon's geography and geology. Detailed maps can make the difference between life and death for some early arrivals. Lunar shadows are completely black, and objects in them are invisible. An astronaut who walks into a shadow may tumble into an unseen pit. And the curve of the lunar surface is so sharp for a man of average height the horizon is only two miles away.

Some day navigational aids and beacons will stud the peaks and craters. Some day roving vehicles and emergency shelters will make a mistaken landmark no more serious than on Earth. But until then, only knowledge will protect men from becoming hopelessly lost. Crewmen afoot on the moon could be in serious trouble trying to decide whether a nameless ridge they see is a half-mile or two miles ahead, and how high it is.

The moonscape is a hodgepodge with some features unlike any on Earth. There are long cracks which have no exact geologic counterparts here; craters of at least five different ages; channels that resemble dry riverbeds; a great straight cliff a thousand feet high; long white streaks radiating like spokes from some of the craters. Many of these streaks are 1,500 miles long, overlaying mountains, dead seas, and craters—which means they must be younger than what they cross. Astronomers are not sure how they got there or what they are made of.

Earth and its constant companion, the moon, are a double planet by astronomical standards, because they are so nearly the same size—unlike all the sun's other planets and moons. These two neighbors are likely to have been formed of the same materials, by the same processes, and during the same time period. So lunar exploration may tell us valuable facts about Earth. For example, no one knows why metallic ores are distributed and concentrated as they are in Earth's crust. Clues revealing the pattern may be found on the moon.

A nearby planet with one-fifth of the land area of Earth, only three days away, demands exploring. The exploration cannot be completed in two or three missions; the moon is fourteen million square miles of new territory, or a larger area than Africa. For Americans not to send expeditions there would leave us like a tribe that stays on its own island and never crosses to the island on the horizon.

Although low-level satellites can map the moon and photograph it, and robots can sample it, geologists on the surface will have to fill in details with hammers and microscopes and drilling rigs. Close-up examination "may permit us to learn," as one geologist said, "how the solar system, the Earth, and the continents on which we live were formed."

The moon is a complete geological record almost undisturbed since its birth billions of years ago. Studying that record can solve the riddle of the moon's age and origin—whether it was once part of Earth and broke off, or was formed separately at the same time and has been Earth's satellite from the beginning, or spent its early youth as an independent planet and later fell captive in Earth's orbit. The chronicle of the lunar surface may even reach back to the birth of our solar system.

Thus it is potentially a much more valuable and informative piece of real estate than it seems at first thought. Hence ten Apollo landings are planned, to be followed by bigger expeditions when the groundwork is laid.

Inevitably, hundreds of Earth dwellers will settle there sooner or later, for the reasons we have seen. But full colonization of the moon may take many decades. Before then—in fact, during the 1970's—many other Earthlings are likely to be living and working off the Earth, in big orbiting Space bases. Almost any of us could conceivably find ourselves in Space some time during the next generation. The next chapter describes why, and how.

11

YOU AND SPACE

●

Are we not now, I sometimes wonder, living in a period of deceptive quiet—the first few seconds, relatively, of the Space Age? In our daily lives few of us are much aware of Space Age problems that demand intelligent answers. . . .

Only now are we beginning to realize the vast economic and social implications of the Space program for the multitude of us who have no present intention of riding a rocket to the moon or Mars.
   —Joseph A. Beirne, President of the Communications
      Workers of America

●

The chance of one of us riding a rocket is greater than we think.

As for our daily life here on Earth, it has already begun to change, because of what men are seeking in Space. It will change more vitally with each passing year, through forces and factors to be scanned later in this chapter. Changes are in the air, coming from Space—changes not only in what we do, and how we do it, but in how we feel about the universe around us.

And there is a real prospect, for one who will live another quarter-century, that he will go up into Space for a pleasure trip, or for his health, or perhaps to earn a living. The rocket he rides is less likely to go to the moon or Mars than to one of the man-made moons that in the 1970's will begin to spangle the skies a few hundred miles above Earth.

The orbiting Space base, or permanent manned moonlet, is the logical next step after the early reconnaissance of the moon. Plans for the first such islands in Space—and some actual structures for them—have been in development since 1963; our earliest islands themselves are scheduled to rise into place, ready for occupancy, starting in late 1971. Some of these will be part of NASA's post-Apollo plan, often called the Apollo Application Program (AAP).

Astronauts who take up residence in Space—at first for only a month at a time, then for longer periods—may be as cramped as submariners, until the second or third generations of Space stations come along. Their first home-above-home will probably be the size of a small house trailer (about 25 feet long and 10 feet wide), or perhaps twice that if it is part of AAP. NASA intends first to use the three-man Apollo spacecraft developed for the moon voyages, and then probably the refurbished empty shell of a Saturn launching rocket's third stage, which is about as roomy as a small bungalow.

These, of course, are byproducts of the billions already spent on our Space program. About nine-tenths of the designs developed for Saturn, Gemini, and Apollo are thus a long-term basic resource that can be used continuously. Aerospace contractors need only resume production of vehicles they have been building, with minor changes to give these newer versions more elbowroom inside. Most major systems can be left intact.

"What we bought with Apollo," says Bob Thompson, AAP program manager at NASA's Manned Spacecraft Center in Houston, "wasn't just the ability of landing men on the moon. We bought a broad base of technology and competence. AAP is one attempt to utilize this base in developing further capabilities in Space."

The inhabitants of Space stations will work in shirtsleeve ease in a weightless wonderland with no up or down, no seasons or weather, night changing to day every few hours.

The phenomenon of "zero gravity" is misunderstood by many

people. In a Space station or a ship coasting between Earth and the moon, gravity's pull is not much lessened. The reason astronauts feel weightless is because they are no longer resisting gravity. Anyone feels weightless on Earth in an elevator that is dropping fast. An orbiting station is always dropping freely—not toward Earth but around it. The astronauts can walk on walls and ceilings with virtually no effort, or propel themselves across the room with a gentle shove. They can stand on either side of a see-through metal grid floor. They dine without need of napkins; exhaust fans suck out any floating food particles. There will be a forced-air toilet, and a wardroom for relaxation. Shaving and sponge baths, troublesome chores on the early manned flights, will present no problems. Sleep will be marvelously comfortable, floating in mid-cabin.

What will these Space dwellers do? Why does the government plan to settle them in such strange outposts? One reason is to enhance the chances for world peace.

The prospects of avoiding an arms race in Space seem promising. In September 1963 the Soviet Union joined the US and the other members of the Eighteen-Nation Committee on Disarmament in sponsoring the so-called "no bombs in orbit" resolution. This resolution, together with the agreement that bans test explosions in Space as well as in the atmosphere, may go far toward eliminating the threat of nuclear war. The Soviet government has lately given up its habit of parading atomic weapons through Red Square.

America has the know-how and much of the hardware to establish its own 30-person station, whenever funds become available. Six Apollo or Gemini-type craft can be docked together to make an "instant Space station," as advocates call it. Therefore various sets of Gemini and Apollo capsules and Saturn rocket stages may be orbiting workships of astronauts for the next decade or more and may be the nuclei around which bigger and bigger satellites are built section by section—just as on Earth great capitals grew from ancient villages or fortified camps. The orbital cities will be constructed from materials manufactured there or on the moon, or ferried from Earth by relays of freighter rockets, which can dump loads in Space to be used later as needed. The parts will be assembled by men in Space suits or tiny spacecraft, propelled by low-powered rocket jets so they can move about easily.

Our first stations will be used, among other things, as way stations for the moon and launch pads for missions deeper into Space. A ship launched from the flywheel of an already speeding orbital platform will not need nearly as huge rockets as those of Saturn V, particularly since there is no air friction to overcome. Hence it is an ideal springboard both for robot probes and for manned expeditions.

Just as the air age sprouted airports, the age of Space travel will require cosmodromes near Earth (and near the moon too, a bit later). A shuttle ship could rocket up from Earth, dock at the station's hangar, and discharge passengers through a telescoping airlock into a waiting room. While the travelers wait for their connecting flight to the moon or elsewhere, the shuttle ship would refuel for its back to Earth, with the crew of the station swarming around in Space like an airport ground crew, or like divers around a submarine.

A nuclear-powered ferry (carring 28 passengers, according to one design on the drawing boards of a NASA contractor) can take passengers and cargo to the vicinity of the moon, then ease into lunar orbit and debark them into a landing craft for the hundred-mile trip down to the moon's surface. Many of us will live to see a time when scientists travel back and forth to the moon as casually as they now jet overseas. In fact, Dr. Wernher von Braun, director of NASA's Space Flight Center, says "some day —and not as far as you might think—there may be tourist flights to the moon."

Space shuttles which can be used repeatedly like aircraft, not jettisoned after every mission, will dramatically cut the costs of Space commuting. The Air Force and NASA have awarded con-

tracts for design studies of three new kinds of rockets for shuttles
—and a fourth, the Aerospike engine, is already in development.
Whichever is chosen will propel a long- sleek, winged vehicle that
will take off from airfields on Earth, climb into Space, and later
reenter the atmosphere and land like a conventional aircraft "in
dignity without splashing," as aerospace engineers say. The famous
X-15 research aircraft, which flew at great heights for eight years
and went as fast as our Mercury manned capsules, gave scientists
many facts and ideas needed for design of a Space shuttle.

Once in production, each shuttle may cost as little as $40 mil-
lion—less than some airlines cost today. This could trim the price
of putting a payload into orbit from today's $500 per pound down
to $50. With new types of engines now under study, the cost
should drop to $10 a pound, Dr. von Braun thinks. "I visualize a
day when everything the U. S. launches is first put on the shuttle,
then sent out from the Space station," says Thomas O. Paine,
who was named to head NASA in March, 1969. "It would be the
low-cost way to open up the moon for exploration and exploita-
tion."

It would also provide money-saving shortcuts to exploration of
the planets. This may be Moscow's reason for pushing development of orbiting stations rather than new Space ships. In 1969
the chairman of the Soviet Council for Internation Cooperation
in the Investigation and Utilization of Outer Space said in a
statement circulated by the Russians that the USSR was focusing
its efforts on Space stations for exploration of the universe. One
US scientist, at least, is sure that the Soviets will send a manned
expedition to circumnavigate Mars three to five years before we
do. Several Russians recently emerged from a sealed chamber with
self-contained life-support systems after a year—the duration of a
voyage to Mars. The position of Earth and Mars will be favorable
for such a mission in 1973, and America and Russia have both
sent unmanned picture-taking craft as necessary preliminaries.

Planetary exploration may last for centuries. Meanwhile the
orbiting Space stations which are steppingstones to the planets will

have been growing steadily. In the next six years, in fact, they should grow to habitations for minimum crews of nine. NASA has asked for bids on the design and construction of such structures, and has announced that it seeks to orbit these stations in the mid-1970's.

Before then, if all goes well, NASA crews of at least three men will have lived in smaller Space bases for 56-day tours of duty some 200 miles above Earth. In such a low orbit, they can be provided with roomy quarters and a well-stocked laboratory simply by using the lifting power of the Saturn V rockets we already have.

In the later 1970's, NASA is expected to put up a big "orbiting campus" that will stay in place for ten years, with twelve-man crews changing every six months. Eventually the campus can be expanded to house 100 U.S. and foreign scientists, including women as well as men.

The pace of progress toward such an edifice speeded up in February 1969, when NASA's top Space flight officials met at the agency's research center in Virginia and decided to go straight to development of the 100-man station, leapfrogging past an intermediate series of smaller Space bases they had previously visualized. The new plan called for establishing the first section of the huge platform, with as many as twelve astronauts in it, by 1975, and a gradual buildup to the three-section island by 1980. Qualified bidders in the aerospace industry were given nine-month study contracts for this giant project in 1969. If Congress approves, actual designing and construction may be under way by the time you read this.

Whether Space stations of the 1970's are small or large, they will serve many practical purposes. Many of the unmanned satellites discussed in other chapters could be even more useful as part of a manned Space station complex. Robot sensing systems cannot decide which areas are most important and often transmit much of the same data over and over. A trained human observer could concentrate on findings of special interest, focus more instruments quickly, and ignore whatever is less important or store it in computer memories for leisurely study later. He could also make repairs. (The failure of the first $69 million Orbiting Astronomical Observatory in 1966 could have been repaired by a man aboard with a screwdriver.)

A man in a Space station may do, in a few days, some jobs that take months or years when tons of robot-reported sensings must be sifted. His on-the-spot decisions may significantly speed the work of spaceborne sensors in improving harvests all over the world, foretelling crop yields, spotting plant diseases, mapping ocean currents, pinpointing sources of air and water pollution, finding underground water and precious deposits, minimizing flood and storm damages through early warnings. International Business Machine engineers say that an orbiting laboratory might complete in two days a global survey taking years by other means.

Someday we will dial an Environmental Forecast Center for an exact prediction of the weather on any future day, any place on Earth. That Center will probably get its information from offices in Space where a few highly trained meteorologists correlate data from weather satellites and ground stations all over the globe, and take their own special observations whenever advisable.

The average person will certainly know more about the universe than the great astronomers know today, if he merely reads some of the press features that are bound to appear soon after Space stations begin mounting astronomical instruments—13 of which are due to go up with the third crew to enter NASA's first station.

Orbiting telescopes, while not the equal of those we shall eventually fix firmly on the moon, will nevertheless make Earthbound observatories obsolete. No air will blur the view in Space. Nor will observers have to stop work, as Earthbound astronomers must, when clouds splotch the sky; all clouds will be far below them. A Space platform can erect giant floating mirrors scores of feet across, supported only by spidery scaffolding, since weight will not matter. (A radio telescope about twelve miles across has also been proposed.) Within its first months a mere 36-inch in orbit can vastly multiply our knowledge of the planets, which will loom ten times closer and fifty times sharper. We need this knowledge before venturing onward to Mars and Venus.

An orbiting base may also prove invaluable as a repair station. Today, spinning endlessly and uselessly around Earth, dozens of unmanned satellites have ceased to send signals. A manned station may be able to seek out some of these dead robots almost automatically, lock onto them, and restore them to useful life. Satellites in higher orbits can be serviced by crews sent up from the station in low-powered shuttles.

Some crewmen will also be trained in factory technology, and will experiment to learn how Space's unique conditions can best be used in manufacturing processes. Space is a better vacuum than can be provided on Earth; even a small vacuum chamber here is hard to build and costly to maintain, because of troublesome leaks. Electronic welding, which works best in a vacuum, is likewise limited and expensive on Earth, but a simpler job in Space. Early tests in the orbiting workshop will assess the feasibility of using an electron beam gun to weld antennae and other parts of big structures in Space.

Other tests in this weird workshop will exploit freedom from gravity. Molten metal, floating in Space, shapes itself into a perfect sphere; bubbles of liquid don't bounce and seldom break; bubbles of air and other gases can be evenly distributed inside liquids of all kinds.

One result may be ball bearings more perfectly round than any made on Earth, which could greatly lengthen the life of many kinds of rotary machines. Another result may be a steel foam almost as light as balsa yet strong and heat-resistant as steel. Still another could be big perfect lenses or mirrors, painfully difficult to manufacture on Earth but essential in some optical instruments.

Metallurgists may concoct wonder metals, since differences in specific gravities will no longer be troublesome in mixing liquids and blending uniform alloys. The simple act of embedding fibers of strong material in a weaker one is known to impart unaccustomed robustness to almost any soft and ductile metal. But aligning the filaments evenly through the metal, and making them adhere, have been so difficult that metal workers do not yet make much use of this ancient principle. They think the embedding and spacing will be easy in a gravity-free shop. If so, phenomenally strong and light materials will come down from Space. Through their use airplanes may be lighter, turbine engines may blast out more power, suspension bridges may be twice as long as today's longest, and skyscrapers may tower five times taller than the Empire State Building.

Such research is scheduled and budgeted for the first phase of NASA's Product Manufacturing in Space program, due to start in August 1971 aboard an orbital laboratory made from one of the giant Saturn fuel tanks left over in Space after its jettisoning in an Apollo launch. In a later phase, eagerly awaited by medical men, there will be experiments with massive electron microscopes (which can magnify alone in a vacuum). On Earth, researchers cannot rely on the electron beam to get sharp pictures with high magnification, because any Earthly vacuum has a few left-over particles of air that deflect some of the electrons. In a Space laboratory, unimagined discoveries may become visible through these microscopes, which can magnify 200,000 times and are therefore our chief means of studying bacteria and viruses.

These are some of the ways the work in Space can influence our lives within the next few years. We have already benefited from offshoots of the preparations to put men into Space: miniaturized electronic systems, new food-treatment methods, nonflammable fabrics and paints, freezer-to-oven-to-table serving dishes, remote-control devices for television sets and for garage doors—the list could go on indefinitely. In industry, some assembly lines are now regulated automatically by voice command, and rockets first designed for spacecraft are used deep underground in mining very hard iron ore which is expected to provide industry with one-third of its ores by 1980. In medicine, some of the benefits were mentioned in Chapter 10; further, doctors are learning how to use microelectronics in a person's body to sharpen his senses, take over body functions, and increase strength and mobility. Out of Space research are coming instruments that have already enabled some invalids to walk, the totally deaf to hear, the voiceless to talk.

Doctors and hospitals can treat ills more accurately with help from computerized diagnosis and electronic data-handling systems that give instant access to tabulations of many similar case histories. Soon a hospital patient, wearing a tiny transmitter on his arm or leg, may call for help even before he realizes he needs it; such units already are used to sense six different physiological conditions, print them out on the kind of strip-charts used daily by doctors, and even flash red-light warnings when advisable.

A more spectacular advance in medical treatment is in prospect for the 1980's or 1990's: an orbital hospital. Krafft A. Ehricke, a far-thinking scientist at North American Rockwell, has already sketched a 150-bed Space hospital. It would have ladder-like wings, with each rung on the ladder serving as a separate ward. The wings would revolve like a huge windmill, to create varying degrees of synthetic gravity. As a person moved toward the hub and the speed of rotation slowed, the gravity would weaken as well, leaving him weightless at the center.

When we progress far enough to be able to move patients to such a hospital without overstress from launch acceleration (they would be under deep anesthesia, of course) they will get medical advantages no billionaire can buy on Earth. Think how weightlessness would ease the burden on the heart, since it would not need to pump as hard to force blood up and down the body. Think how treatment of severe burns and recuperation from all sorts of injuries could be speeded, when the patient floats freely instead of lying on his dressings or his injuries. Bedsores would not exist. Flesh would not sag. Without skeletal tension and compression, pinched nerves and slipped spinal discs could be relieved at once.

Medical lore tells of a little girl in an elevator, where a big piece of candy lodged in her windpipe. The alarmed elevator operator started down at maximum speed—virtually a free fall. In the few seconds of near weightlessness, the candy floated free and the girl breathed. The examining doctor remarked that there were times in every operation when he wished he could have his patient in that elevator, just to cancel the pressure of gravity on vital organs.

A rest home in Space could be a permanent haven for the crippled and infirm, since they would no longer need crutches or wheelchairs. They could dive, float, sail, and roll languorously at will, and move from place to place with a fingertip push. Their lives could be far more self-reliant and useful than on Earth.

Indeed, it may turn out that anyone can live longer when not glued down by gravity nor exposed to the infections and contagions of Earth. People may not need so much sleep, thanks to the reduced physical strains. We may find all old folks who can afford it rushing out to health resorts in Space. One of the burning social questions of the next generation, if Space really proves a key to longer life, will be the question of how to select the lucky ones to go there.

An orbital hotel, with variable-gravity suites and possibilities for exhilarating new kinds of recreation, was seriously discussed at a 1967 symposium on "Commercial Uses of Space." The speaker was Barron Hilton, who knows a good deal about hotels. "If the world powers continue to restrict outer Space to peaceful pursuits, there will be travelers in Space," he said. "And where there are travelers, there must be Hiltons."

At a Space hotel we might step from our artificial-gravity room into recreation rooms where we weighed little or nothing. There might be one called a Dynarium in which vacationers would float and tumble in circulating air currents, or bounce from wall to wall, cushioned by nets and rubber linings, in a kind of three-dimensional trampoline. A swimming pool could be a giant bubble—really a hollow ball of water, with an air space in the center. Or it could have a curved surface, so we would float in the trough of a great motionless wave. Outside there might be facilities for Space excursion boats and for walks in Space suits with tethers. We may find ourselves, as Saint-Exupéry wrote in another context, "solemnly taking our constitutional between Sagittarius and the Great Bear.

"I personally think we will find that the environment of Space is the easiest environment man has ever encountered, once you pay the price of admission," says Stark Draper, director of the Massachusetts Institute of Technology's Instrumentation Laboratory and one of the world's leading aeronautical engineers.

A good part of that price has already been paid. Of all the billions we spent on the Space program, only about $2 billion (for the "Snoopy" moon-landing ferry) were exclusively for lunar operations. The rest bought the huge launch facilities, rocket-testing stands, guidance systems, control mechanisms, spacecraft factories, skilled technicians, scientific knowledge, and other assets that are needed whatever the goal in Space. The eight-year drive for the moon fed on virtually the entire range of science from astronomy to zoology, forcing scientists to advance on many frontiers, and forcing organizations to develop almost every facet of Space capability needed for habitable satellites as well as for planetary exploration.

One cost-cutting step often advocated now, particularly by military men, is to combine the Air Force and NASA programs in Space to avoid duplication. "It is imperative that we call a halt to this duplication, and concentrate on the Air Force program," said Republican Congressman John Wydler as the new Nixon Administration prepared to take office. He was elaborating an argument advanced earlier by retired Air Force General Bernard A. Schriever, famed as a leader in developing ballistic missiles:

The arbitrary separation of Space activities into peaceful and military is just that—arbitrary. It simply serves to emphasize by comparison the straightforwardness of the Soviet program.

Their single-purpose program seeks only to attain a versatile technological superiority which, once attained, will serve the political purpose they choose.

Substantial numbers of Congressmen feel that the Air Force should control manned flight activities while NASA should stick to scientific satellites and unmanned Space probes. If this school of thought prevails, a wall of military secrecy will doubtless shut off America's major activities in Space. Dozens of other nations, now helping us and being helped by NASA's work, would be likely to revert to their earlier fears that America meant to master the whole world through Space weaponry. One eminent retired U.S. Army general, James M. Gavin, has warned, "Governments have been toppled and 'good' nations have been conquered and destroyed because they followed the advice of their military experts."

Our peaceful uses of Space in the past decade have brought nations much closer in kinship. But if all our ships and stations in Space are under Air Force orders, the effect on international friendship may be much the same as if we mounted cannons on our jetliners, fortified our embassies, and put colonels in command of them. Every one who hopes that Space will help man rise above warfare may be well advised to oppose the Pentagon's push for dominance there.

So far President Nixon has seemed cool to unification maneuvers, just as his three immediate predecessors did. President Eisenhower took the firmest stand of all when, in 1960, he told Congress that the concept of "a single program embracing military as well as nonmilitary activities in Space should be eliminated."

As Joseph Beirne indicated in the quotation that opens this chapter, many indirect consequences of the Space Age are scarcely noticeable in our daily lives, yet have deep hidden significance for us. Less dramatic than the mighty rocket's blasts, the secondary consequences are more fundamental, spreading like earthquake tremors to the roots of our society.

One of these consequences is the sharp, continuing stimulus to factories and corporations all over America. As Lloyd V. Berkner, one of the planners of the International Geophysical Year, pointed out in 1966, "By setting our Space goals at the limits of our capability, we have created standards of technological perfection that challenge equal perfection by every industry in our land. These new standards are being felt by every man—in new levels of productivity, new products and services that are making possible our ever-more-affluent technological society." Fully a third of today's products did not exist in 1960. And we can be rather sure that a third of everything sold today will soon be obsolete.

The new standards are also felt in the way men work with each other. The Space program was the first big industrial effort in history not accompanied by a need for mountains of mass-produced materials—and thus by a need for armies of people on standardized assembly lines. Its great demand, instead, was for skills and devotion. To make a Space bird fly, every one of thousands of people had to do superlative work.

Most people work well only if they know they are needed and their work is important. In high-technology companies there has long been a shortage of capable labor and management; therefore anyone who found his job dull has simply moved to another company. Consequently managers have had to learn to give workers a new picture of themselves as creative, useful people instead of tiny faceless pawns. Moreover, when problems arose, managers found that a good way to solve them was to discuss them openly with everyone concerned—which would have been unthinkable in most companies as recently as 1960. This new openness changed some managements from top to bottom, and changed workers.

In short, the old-fashioned pyramid structure of business organization began to crumble. It was too rigid and sluggish to adapt to the pell-mell changes of fast-developing Space projects. A centralized decision-maker was apt to wave away a new idea because he was too busy to understand it—and new ideas are the lifeblood of Space work.

For simple tasks under static conditions a whip-cracking Big Boss is probably more efficient. But for adaptability to change, for quick grasp of new ideas, for the high morale needed in dealing with unfamiliar problems, decentralized and more democratic kind of organization has evolved in countless corporations. Subordinates with dissenting views are encouraged to speak up. On programs such as Apollo, it is not enough to snatch up the first solution to a problem that appears. Because of the risks and unknowns, every alternative solution or opinion must be considered carefully. Space work is a great environment for free thinkers.

The trend to democratization and "participative management," as it is often called, has been spreading gradually but surely. Industrial giants are splitting up monolithic management structures into something like separate businesses within the business. And their departments are no longer rigidly compartmentalized; there are "many more fluid, adaptive, temporary groups within the company," to quote a recent article in a management magazine. Flexibility and creativity are the new watchwords.

As this trend deepens, today's hot competition for capable employees will seem tepid. There will be an upswing in salaries and fringe benefits, and in benefits not directly taxable. There will be ardent wooing of new managerial sources such as women, younger employees, and ethnic minorities. There will be much stronger emphasis on identifying promotable personnel. In short, Space is transforming corporations into much more stimulating places to work. The trend may be a long time reaching companies that manufacture toothpicks or shoelaces, but even such firms may have so much difficulty attracting new employees that they eventually humanize themselves.

Another indirect consequence of man's leap toward the planets has been the emergence of massive, intricate programs calling for close cooperation between hundreds of contractors, suppliers, scientific instiutuions, and government bureaus. Factory bosses, accustomed to ruling little kingdoms of their own, have had to become perceptive and flexible in working with similar monarchs above, below, and around them. Every year more organizations are dependent on each other.

Likewise the "multidisciplinary approach" to problem-solving has forced engineers to make themselves understood by physicists and vice versa; chemists have had to team up with psychologists; astronomers descend from observatories to help geologists climbing up from caves. It is no longer safe to say that a specialist is a man who knows more and more about less and less.

By the same token, we all are learning more. Suddenly biology, electronics, meterology, navigation, metallurgy, geography, sociology and countless other branches of knowledge are in the news. They touch our lives and our futures. To understand our modern world, let alone act in it, we find ourselves busy with continuous, informal self-education—for fun as well as for profit. Some 200, 000 Americans started flying lessons in 1969, nearly quadruple the 1961 level.

Our first-graders will be able to fly to the moons of Jupiter in middle age. And we ourselves may retool for a totally different kind of work any day now. Some 70 per cent of the skilled trades in American industry in 1900 have vanished today. It is a safe bet that most of today's skills will become obsolete before we retire, while technological change opens up new occupations at a dizzy rate.

According to a former U.S. Commissioner of Education, Harold Howe, "Most people will have jobs that will change in nature two or three times during their lifetime. Education has the obligation to enable them to make these occupational changes." Studying recent statistics, employment agencies estimate that more than half of last June's graduates will switch jobs at least once in the first five years out of college, a mobility unprecedented in history. Lifelong learning, then, is part of the quickening pace of the Space Age. Educators are advocating educational systems that are "open-ended, with freedom for mature students to enter, leave, and reenter at will."

12

HOW SPACE IS CHANGING
THE WORLD

●

*The beeps that come to us from our satellites in chill and
distant Space tell us something vastly more important than
the secrets of the ionosphere. They tell us that this tiny
globe that we inherit has become so diminished that every
man is in fact every man's next-door neighbor.*
—Whitney M. Young, Jr.

●

The Kremlin phoned the White House, asking to be kept informed via the Washington-Moscow hot line; and the President's
staff did so. Meanwhile history's biggest television audience stared
at pictures broadcast live to networks across Europe, Japan, and
North and Central and South America. What was happening?
What conceivable event could catch interest around the world,
among statesmen and housewives and peons alike?

The event, of course, was the epochal voyage of Apollo 8 in
Christmas week of 1968: a long-awaited journey unlike any before
it in Earth's long history. For seven years *genus homo* had edged
into the eternal cold of Space, soaring as high as 853 miles above

the ground. Now at last he was making the great escape from his own planet. Reporters from forty nations gathered at Cape Kennedy to watch the mighty rocket rise.

The astronauts Borman, Anders, and Lovell were fulfilling mankind's oldest dream and universal myth. The urge to soar free, to explore the unknown, to visit another celestial body, is as old as the legends of Icarus and Diana. People of all kinds have this in common, and so on December 21, 1968 their hearts soared into Space, following the rocket on its long wild way to the moon.

As President Johnson remarked afterward, "For seven days the Earth and all who inhabit it knew a measure of unity through these brave men. . . . These men represented in the vastness of Space all mankind, all its races, all its nationalities, all its religions, all its ideologies."

On their translunar passage the astronauts aimed a television camera and sent back stunning pictures of a great heavenly body no man had ever seen before—because none had ever left it. And as the state of Texas, Florida, California, or Alaska vanished into cloud seas—as the United States shrank to a misted island, as Africa and Europe and Asia merged and the entire planet Earth became a single lovely sphere—the sight set many people to thinking one thought.

The thought was best expressed, perhaps, by the poet Archibald MacLeish: "To see the Earth as it truly is . . . is to see ourselves as riders on the Earth together, brothers on that bright loveliness in the eternal cold—brothers who know now they are truly brothers." Others said the same in different words. A German lecturer in war studies at the University of London wrote: "The remarkable pictures of the Earth taken from near the moon's surface impress on us the utter ridiculousness of the nature and substance of man's quarrels with man . . . and the tendency, particularly among younger people, to see the world's problems as a whole, regardless of national or regional confines." Norman Cousins, widely known editor and worker for peace, wrote:

"It is possible that the most effective and imaginative thing the United States could do at Paris (in the Vietnam war negotiations) would be to send over the astronauts of Apollo 8 as our negotiators. The astronauts have seen the Earth whole, something the statesmen have yet to do."

As the dreaming moon raced below them on Christmas Eve, the astronauts talked and the world heard. Space, hundreds of thousands of miles of Space, and these voices pulsing through it, finding their way back to Earth and quickening men's hearts.

What could the astronauts say at this milestone in history, as the human family felt itself moving toward a strange new destiny? What would be worth hearing by the peoples of the globe with their parliaments, their temples, their armies, their corporations, their farms? Bill Anders wrote later:

> We thought a long time about that, and I personally changed my mind. I first thought we should use something Christian, something about Christmas. But when we thought about the vastness of our world, we decided to read a message that did not belong to any one religion but which belonged to all men on Earth, the story of our creation.

And so the astronauts spoke perhaps the most fitting words imaginable, the majestic opening passage of the Book of Genesis: "In the beginning God created . . . "

And Frank Borman signed off with a prayer: "O God . . . show us what each of us can do to set forth the coming of the day of universal peace."

These religious thoughts, at the height of a great scientific mission, proved to be widely shared. It was remarkable how this crossing of Space turned men's minds inside out, away from intramural struggles, toward human brotherhood and toward a God whose unimaginable complexity had generated galaxies and atoms and thinking humans. The Astronauts' humble words were rebroadcast in many languages over radio networks in the free world and Communist world alike. Even Red Hungary, one of the most totalitarian of governments, interrupted its radio and television programs for Apollo broadcasts.

As the little ship completed its ten orbits of the moon and turned homeward, a top Soviet Space scientist told newsmen, "This goes beyond a national achievement. It marks a stage in the development of the universal culture of Earthmen." And when the ship came down from the silent gulfs of Space and landed safe on Earth again, a wave of joy ran around the globe. Warm messages poured in by the thousands to the Manned Spacecraft Center in Texas. Ten Soviet cosmonauts wired congratulations, concluding: "We wish you further success on all other flights. We are confident future exploration of Space will greatly benefit Earthly men."

An American foreign correspondent reported from Paris: "Moon flight has changed the atmosphere. Americans on the streets, in the shops, everywhere, get French congratulations." A reporter in London wrote, "The American public performance invites the whole world to take part."

The invitation was reiterated and stressed in Washington. As he presented medals to the returned spacefarers, President Johnson said:

We have learned how men and nations may make common cause in the most magnificent and hopeful enterprises.

We in the United States are already engaged in cooperative space activities with more than 70 nations. We have proposed a variety of adventures to expand international partnership in Space exploration.

. . . If there is an ultimate truth to be learned from this historic flight, it may be this: There are few social or scientific or political problems which cannot be solved by men, if they truly want to solve them together.

The same fraternal thought bloomed in a speech by a State

Department dignitary, Robert F. Packard, director of a comparatively new and little-known agency, the Office of Outer Space Affairs:

> Encouraging others to participate in our Space program should demonstrate that our approach to the changing world is responsive to their interests as well as our own. Thus we seek international arrangements for the conduct of activities in Space. . . .

> We intend that Space exploration be handled so as to avoid the inequities and international fragmentation which accompanied seaborne explorations 400 years ago. We should seek every possible means to relate it, not only to our own needs, but to the real interests of others. This means finding meaningful opportunities for foreign participation—direct or indirect. It means coordinated, or joint, efforts with others wherever reasonable and possible.

Even as he spoke, the tangled politics of diplomacy were loosening perceptibly in the flood of good will. Apollo and Kosmos and Tiros and their myriad companions overhead had blown down fences that had stood for decades or centuries. A quiet transformation in international affairs was speeding up, with subtle impacts on human society and perhaps even on human nature. The change was already in progress years ago, when the moon seemed very far away, and will continue for decades to come. No historic mutation occurs overnight, and of course many other factors besides Space exploration have contributed.

As tiny indicators of the deep shift, some simple semantic questions may be revealing: How long has it been since we last saw Africa described as the Dark Continent? How long since we heard anyone speak of an Iron Curtain? For that matter, have we heard the Cold War mentioned lately?

The first gentle unifying tugs of the Space Age were felt in 1954, even before the first proof that a man-made object could ascend into Space and stay put. At that time scientists from 72 nations were sketching the most intricate global research effort yet conceived: The International Geophysical Year, scheduled for 1957-58. This was a civilian enterprise nurtured by the United Nations and aimed at learning more about our planet—not only its structure, interior, and surface, but also its mysterious upper atmosphere and its role in the universe. The U.S. Committee of the IGY organization suggested that, as part of the nation's share in the vast project, a satellite be launched. The government approved this heady plan; the White House announced it to a skeptical and heedless world. A day later the USSR declared that it too would put up a satellite for the IGY.

Most observers assumed that if any satellite ever actually got into orbit, Americans would be the launchers, because of America's acknowledged engineering supremacy. But in October 1957, three months after the IGY began, the Soviets utterly astounded the world by orbiting the first artificial satellite. It weighed 184 pounds and bristled with instruments to measure and relay data on pressures and temperatures.

That was the day Space got into international politics. The USSR was accused of having jumped the gun, of having kept its plan secret in order to gain propaganda advantage from surprise. Soviet scientists retorted that they had kept IGY headquarters in Brussels advised of progress, and that anyone could deduce from their reports that the countdown was planned for somewhere around October.

Nevertheless this feat by the Soviet Union, followed in 119 days by the first tiny US Satellite, turned scientific cooperation into Cold War scrambling. Sputnik's size was ominous evidence that it was launched not by a small, purely scientific rocket but by a launcher big enough to hurl intercontinental bombs. This seemed to open the much-discussed "missile gap" and led to the speed-up of military rocket tests. The continuing IGY satellite programs raised specters of Space mines, orbiting weapons, spies in the sky, and forts on the moon.

To calm these fears President Eisenhower sent Lyndon B. Johnson, then a Senator, before the General Assembly of the United Nations to say:

> To keep Space as man has found it and to harvest the yield of peace which it promises, we of the United States see one course—and only one—which the nations of Earth may intelligently pursue. That is the course of full and complete and immediate cooperation to make the exploration of outer Space a joint adventure.

Eisenhower also set up a new government agency, the National Aeronautics (curiously old-fashioned word!) and Space Administration, to conduct most of the nation's Space missions. The President explained that he wanted a civilian-run rather than a military agency "because it is of great importance to have the fullest cooperation of the scientific community at home and abroad. Moreover a civilian setting will emphasize the concern of our nation that Space be devoted to peaceful and scientific purposes." Some day historians may decide that this choice by the old general led mankind safely past a fateful crossroads.

In Congress both political parties saw the perils of extending the Cold War beyond the planet. The National Aeronautics and Space Act of 1958 stipulated that US expertise in Space "should be devoted to peaceful purposes for the benefit of all mankind" and channeled toward "cooperation with other nations and groups of nations." The UN took the same tack. It formed a Committee on the Peaceful Uses of Outer Space, to draft a framework of international law governing the exploration and use of Space, and to encourage the pooling of energies in those cosmic deeds.

Within a few years scores of spacecraft were aloft—some to travel a thousand years, some to go out 42 million miles, some to spin around the sun at 18 miles per second. Men (and a woman) had adventured in Space. Engineers could design and place satellites more or less at will, to aid navigation and communication and to extend the scrutinies IGY had begun of weather, natural resources, and invisible forces outside the atmosphere.

Such pioneering was essentially supranational, since an orbiting spacecraft harms nobody, plunders no treasure, and knows no national boundaries. In March 1959 the United States proclaimed that NASA stood ready to package payloads of mutual interest for other nations. Soon it was receiving foreign proposals and putting some into action.

Little by little, almost unnoticed outside scientific circles, nations widened their horizons and worked together to reap data from Space. They may have shivered and drawn back in 1961 when President Kennedy challenged the US to commit itself to a manned lunar landing as a prime national objective, in order "to become the world's leading spacefaring nation." Perhaps this grated on foreign ears. But Kennedy soon had second thoughts about the likely consequences of flag-waving and muscle-flexing in Space. He publicly avowed faith "that Space can be explored and mastered without feeding the fires of war, without repeating the mistakes that man has made in extending his writ around this globe of ours." He proffered assistance in tracking Soviet manned flights, and suggested cooperative tracking and data-gathering. Moscow balked. Its hidden Space projects were not for sharing.

Two months before his death in 1963, in a speech to the UN General Assembly, Kennedy urged a joint American-Russian effort to get men to the moon. President Johnson later reaffirmed the offer, and made the point plainer: "The race in which we of this generation are determined to be first is the race for peace." There was no official Soviet response. But a Russian cosmonaut told a Havana audience that the Soviet team had already been picked to plant the hammer and sickle on the moon.

Yet Moscow's suspicions and secrecy had evidently been thawing a little, perhaps because NASA kept announcing launches in advance and hiding neither flops nor triumphs. When Khrushchev made a pious mention of the need for cooperation in Space, Kennedy took him at his word and sent specific proposals for cooperation. Russian and American scientists nervously conferred, and eventually agreed on four projects for combined or at least coordinated experiments in meteorology, precision mapping, communication, and Space medicine. These ventures are still inching ahead.

A clearer sign of the Kremlin thaw came in 1965, when a French system in a Russian satellite began beaming color television from Moscow to Paris. In 1966—the year de Gaulle went to Moscow—the Soviets signed a cautious agreement for "scientific and technological cooperation between France and the USSR for the study and peaceful exploration of Space." The agreement specified teamwork in using spacecraft for weather probes as well as for communication. Even more benignly, the Kremlin hitched together a Soviet Council for International Cooperation in the Investigation and Utilization of Outer Space; and in 1967 when the International Astronautical Federation met in deviationist Yugoslavia, Russian Space scientists nevertheless showed up and traded information freely with American colleagues.

Eleven European governments had already been transplanting talents and hardware for various Space tasks since 1960, and in 1966 a broad new secretariat, the European Space Conference, had gone to work on behalf of 19 nations. The 19 included no Communist countries, but left out few others; even the Vatican State and little Monaco joined—and so did Canada and Australia, perhaps considering themselves European in spirit if not in site. Meanwhile NASA's international projects were ushering 69 different nations into Space.

Hence this lofty new dimension of governmental affairs was comfortable for most statesmen by 1967, when the diplomats of 84 nations—including the US and Russia—amicably agreed to an Outer Space Treaty. It forbids military outposts on the moon and planets, outlaws orbiting weapons, and stipulates that Space shall be the "province of all mankind," with no sovereignty to be claimed by any nation. The treaty was endorsed unanimously by the US Senate as well as the UN General Assembly, in a rare and heartening display of concord. During the treaty-signing at the White House, Soviet Ambassador Dobrynin spoke optimistically of Space exploration as "a new idea capable of uniting the thoughts of people all over the Earth," and President Johnson responded that "the great Space armadas of the future will go forth on voyages of peace—and go forth in a spirit not of national rivalry but of peaceful cooperation."

Perhaps the Soviets have grown less fearful and more fraternal because their reconnaissance satellites, like ours, now scrutinize the whole Earth, photographing all warlike works in enlightening detail. Washington's advance announcement of China's would-be secret nuclear tests proved that frontiers are transparent to the spaceborne monitors. Years ago President Johnson said, "If we had no justification for the Space program other than photography, it would be worth ten times the money. I know how many missiles the enemy has." His knowledge saved taxpayers an enormous sum, since the Pentagon could slow down its missile buildup in the certainty that the Kremlin was not deploying rockets as menacingly as had been feared.

Similar knowledge about us has probably soothed Moscow in recent years. Now that it sees for itself, through its Kosmos orbiters, that we are ready to hit back but are not massing for a sneak attack, it may not feel so distrustful as it did in past decades. Who would have thought, when Eisenhower made his noble Open Skies proposal in 1955, that by 1967 it would be an accomplished fact without a parley, without a treaty? Space science has left the superpowers no choice but to live together in an increasingly open world. And openness can only serve the cause of peace.

It does not guarantee universal peace, of course. Recent wars in the Middle East, Africa, and Southeast Asia show that factions may still fight, just as factions in any small town. But in the 1960's other nations have tried to be peacemakers wherever war has broken out or has threatened. Now that television can show everyone, in his own living room, the horror of war while it is happening, peace crusades have waxed far more militant than anyone might have predicted a decade ago.

Indeed, the filters are vanishing between mankind and everything that happens on or around Earth. Consider for a moment what Whitney Young meant, in the quotation that opens this chapter, when he said that the world has diminished. He did not mean—if I may presume to interpret him—that the Pacific is actually narrower or the continents smaller. What is changed is not Earth but Man's knowledge of Earth and man's mobility on Earth. What he knows, and where he goes, encompass the globe. The world has become *our* world in a way it never was before and never could have been. We know now that whatever town, whatever nation we may belong to as citizens, we are bound together in a common fate: the fate of this small planet which is home for us all.

Awareness of the wholeness of Earth, conveyed by the cameras and sensors and television relays in the satellites hundreds of miles above, is steadily unifying the human community. We are reminded almost daily that the other fellow's problems really concern us. And we are showing concern.

For example, the five-year International Biological Program, begun in 1967, unites 50 countries in investigating how the world's plants, animals, soils, climates, peoples, and machines can exist together in a healthy balance. And now Sweden has called urgently for an unprecedented world parley on pollution to be held in 1972 with the UN as impresario. America and the Soviet Union are endorsing the call. They know how efficiently Sweden is coordinating the disposal of its own wastes through its new Nature Management Board; and their sensors in Space show the dire need for similar management on an international scale. In symposium after symposium at the 1969 annual meeting of the American Association for the Advancement of Science, researchers warned of impending calamity as the wastes churned up by man continue to choke the planet.

"Our scientists are well aware of the magnitude of this problem," says Sverker Astrom, Sweden's ambassador to the UN. "But national and international planning is not done by scientists. It is done by politicians."

Yet many politicians (international-type as well as local) are reading the warnings from the sky, and are negotiating agreements to help protect our battered planet. Historically our State Department has not concerned itself much with scientific matters. But now it has an Office of International Scientific and Technological Affairs, headed by an official with rank and authority equal to that of an Assistant Secretary of State; it has a staff of 45 scientists in Washington, and 18 science attachés in US embassies abroad. In fact, every American diplomatic mission in the world is reportedly staffed with at least one aide trained in science and technology. Other nations have also shown their readiness to negotiate on scientific and technological questions by assigning 21 foreign scientific missions to Washington, and by adding science advisers to their diplomatic organizations elsewhere.

Nothing could be more international than weather. Now it is another tie that binds governments together. Simple equipment to absorb data from American (and Russian, since 1966) weather satellites as they whiz overhead has been installed in 382 ground stations scattered across 46 nations. Washington and Moscow share costs of a 24-hour communications link by which they trade all their weather pictures. The newest weather eye, NASA's Nimbus III, circles the globe every 107 minutes, photographing the cloud cover and probing the atmosphere with sophisticated feelers that read temperature, pressure, and humidity up to 30 miles above the ground. The sheer number of its reports is sharply improving the accuracy of weather maps of unpopulated areas—especially the oceans—where few other readings are taken. This helps ships and planes of all nations.

But weather experts not only want more data; they yearn to learn how to use their data. Ignorance of how and why global weather comes and goes is still the big barrier to long-range weather forecasting. To surmount this barrier, 13 nations have teamed in the two-year-old Global Atmospheric Research Program, whose aim is to amass enough knowledge for accurate worldwide 14-day forecasts. In May 1969 the program began its first major test, Project Bomex (for Barbados Oceanographic & Meteorological Experiment), in which 1,500 scientists would pry into conditions over and under 90,000 square miles of Atlantic Ocean for three months. Seven U.S. Government agencies, 19 universities, six industrial laboratories, and the government of Barbados were mobilized in Bomex. Meanwhile the World Weather Watch, described in Chapter 4, got under way in 1968 and will enter its more elaborate second phase in 1972.

Water troubles have bred worldwide interest in the neglected science of hydrology. Under UNESCO sponsorship, scientists from 73 nations began in 1965 to pool their research talents and facilities in the International Hydrological Decade. IHD scientists are deploying a worldwide set of stations to map climate conditions, flash early warnings of floods, study ground-water levels and stream ecology, and measure water's ability to purify itself.

Today almost every branch of science has a foot in Space and is forging new links across international borders. Each year sees at least 30 international conclaves devoted to various aspects of Space science and engineering. The International Committee for Space Research, known as COSPAR, is a federation of 10 scientific societies in 30 countries; several hundred scientists attend its symposium each year. COSPAR sponsors World Data Centers as clearing houses for reports on all kinds of Space experiments.

The compulsion to communicate runs deep in human nature. Long before men discovered electricity, they thought up ways to send messages faster than they could run or ride. They used smoke signals, jungle drums, mirror flashes, belfry lanterns, bugles. So it isn't surprising that they seized on satellites for the same purpose. Today 90 per cent of our international communications are relayed via satellite; a quarter-ton satellite outperforms 150,000 tons of transocean cable. Soon after the US got into Space it set to work on a system of satellites that could receive, amplify, and pass along radio and television signals. This soon led to the remarkable half-public, half-private Communications Satellite Corporation (Comsat), in which many thousands of Americans own stock. Comsat acts as manager of the growing string of satellites governed by an international partnership called Intelsat (for the International Telecommunications Satellite Consortium). Some 67 countries now share ownership of Intelsat. The Communist nations have not joined, but have sent observers, and it seems inevitable that they will be in Intelsat some day—even though the USSR announced in 1968 that it was forming its own rival communications satellite company, Intersputnik.

In a few remote villages across the world, where there are no telephones or tarred roads, there are now satellite receiver stations, each with a loudspeaker and big-screen television. So these villagers are entering the modern world, even if they cannot make a phone call. Their station tells them how to grow more food, how to cook more nourishing meals, how to do the three R's. Within a decade these ground links to the Space Age, now totalling 36, may be counted in the thousands.

By 1971 Comsat hopes to launch the first satellite so powerful that simple home radios can tune in directly, bypassing the ground stations now needed as intermediaries. And by 1975 a satellite may be ready to transmit television into homes. These developments may mean deeper and swifter social changes than did the printing press or railroad. Most new nations already seem to agree that what they chiefly need, more than roads or telephones or even power plants, is schools—and the satellites will provide schooling.

But beyond that, censorship and other barriers to the international flow of information will disappear. No dictator can block the voices from the stars. Thirty years ago the most compelling of revolutionary forces was said to be Hollywood, with its glowing pictures of the abundant life; in the 1970's that force will penetrate far corners it never reached before. Meanwhile doctors and engineers are already beginning to pick up advanced training via satellite, instead of journeying to America or to Europe; exporters and importers use a satellite to telephone the other side of the world to find better deals for their wares, or to buy what they need at lower prices; and governments get extra revenue from the growing volume of international phone calls, telegrams, and teletype services (enough revenue, in fact, to pay for a satellite station in a short time).

America and Europe have seen the homogenizing effects of movies and television on speech, fashion, habits, and attitudes. Less cosmopolitan continents may soon note the same effect from global television. It seems sure to speed the spread of a common language; it may spread ideas even faster. Voices and pictures on television cannot tell us what to think, but they influence what we think about.

Men at sea have long been closer in brotherhood than men behind boundaries; an SOS brings them racing to the rescue regardless of nationality. Now Space engineers have woven other invisible webs of assistance by means of navigation satellites called Transits. Any country's ships and aircraft equipped with the simple receivers needed can use Transits to pinpoint their position. With these satellites, as with our weather satellites and many other Space programs, America is silently saying to every country, every day, that we as a people want to use our new knowledge in a joint effort with them, with benefits for all mankind.

Just as governments are now cooperating in Earth's adventure of self-discovery, so are international business groups. There are organizations like Eurospace and Euratom, associations of manufacturers in the fields of Space equipment and atomic energy. And each year there are more international business ventures. Companies based in the United States have more than fifty billion dollars at work in other countries. Noting this, new nations are so organizing themselves that they can attract private capital from abroad.

The flow of funds is a force for peace. Roger Blough, chairman of US Steel, once pointed out, "Where the economic interest of nationals and of nations are tied together, our broader mutual interests are likely to be bound together also. . . . In a very real sense the multi-nation corporation is the tie that binds." An editorial in *Aviation Week* makes a similar point. "Intergovernmental agreements certainly are necessary to realize the tremendous potential of Space technology. But without the . . . industrial organizations that ultimately have to develop the technology and build the hardware, these official (government) agreements would be more difficult to achieve."

Reaching out from Washington to the ends of the Earth, NASA is zealous and many-sided in its assigned mission of "cooperation with other nations for the benefit of all mankind." It is working with 80 governments from Ascension Island to Zambia in various Space experiments. It exchanges scientific papers with 240 institutions in 41 countries. Each year it launches about 150 sounding rockets in collaborative probes, with other countries, of the layers of airspace above their own lands. It has helped Canada, Japan, France, Germany, and Great Britain design and launch at least 24 satellites.

More than 400 Space scientists and technicians from 14 countries have flocked to America for training in NASA facilities, at their own or their government's expense. NASA's vast variety of off-the-shelf electronic equipment is often rented to foreign experimenters, freeing them from laborious tasks of building their own; and NASA's computers give them quick analyses of experimental results.

In part because of the magnetism of our Space programs, 130,000 foreign students are now in US schools and universities, compared with only 35,000 in 1954. Of these, 1,300 earned Ph.D.'s in Space-related studies in 1968. NASA encouraged their progress by helping universities build research facilities, and sometimes by providing scholarships or research grants.

NASA's beneficences are not one-way. Fifteen countries maintain tracking stations that NASA needs for noting its satellites' courses and performance. Italy's unique San Marco launch platform, peculiarly valuable because it is near the equator, is available to NASA. The European Space Research Organization and 21 nations now trade data with NASA.

Test samples from the moon's surface, borne home by Apollo crews, are to be shared with 135 scientists from 8 foreign countries. In this sense the moon exploration program is truly international. But NASA hopes to be more polyglot still. It wants to enroll men of other countries in the most exclusive and most glamorous apprenticeship the world has ever known: the apprenticeship of NASA astronauts.

When nations do constructive jobs together they brighten the prospects of peace. Their joint activities in Space are among the most hopeful enterprises in history, for they foster world prosperity. A prosperous world tends to be a peaceful world. But beyond their hopes of gain, governments and common people are drawn together by the sheer romantic fascination of thinking about Earthmen on the lunar surface, and of looking ahead up the path to the planets. They feel themselves pulled along by an irresistible historical process, the fulfillment of one era, the dawn of another—an intuitive public certainty that the world has outgrown one way of life and is starting afresh, just as it did when the opening of the New World broke the long imprisonment of the Middle Ages.

13

THE STAR WITHIN

●

It is dangerous to show men too clearly how much he resembles the animal, unless we show him his greatness at the same time. But it is also dangerous to show him his greatness without showing him his baseness. Man is not an angel, and not an animal. It is a misfortune that whoever plays the part of an angel will become an animal.
—Blaise Pascal

●

In this century man has indeed seen how much he resembles the animal: sometimes a mad dog, sometimes a pitiless beast of prey, more often merely a mindless pig wallowing lazily in filth. Amid our abundance we groan at our taxes. Softened by ease and plenty, we begin to show some of the corruption which leisure classes have flaunted throughout history.

Change engulfs us like a torrent. Just consider: in one century technology has swept the common man out of a way of life substantially unchanged since the time of the ancient Egyptians. Within the lifetime of one generation we have moved from the

Steam Age to the Space Age. This generation has had no rest. We have been through a paralyzing worldwide depression, challenged by international fascism and communism, two world wars, the breakup of vast colonial empires, threat of nuclear extermination, the convulsions of a racial revolution. Now we are numbed by assassinations and riots. We seem to be swimming in a millrace with nothing solid underfoot.

But when waters engulf us we reach for a star, as Theodore Dreiser once wrote. The star is within reach. Paracelsus, the Swiss philosopher-physician, reminds us: "Man carries the stars within himself." So let us pause and look—try to get our bearings and find the star.

Almost any citizen of the great modern civilizations can see more of the world in a few weeks than the mightiest emperors of the nineteenth century could see in their lifetimes. Consequently ingrown bias has faded like a nightmare. A century ago a villager might say, "This is how everyone does," when he knew only a handful of people living within a few miles. Today he would never think of saying it. Nor does he think of himself now as someone behind a moat, or on an island, or in the hinterlands. At least people have an image of themselves, of all of us, as men together. Our mastery of flight taught us the wholeness of the Earth, and this has made war far less acceptable.

The crabbed adage, "What was good for our fathers is good enough for us," sounds foolish now. The world of our fathers has vanished. Its disappearance shook our churches. The changes the next decade may bring to established Western religions are beyond imagination.

Of course man's religious ideas have often shifted before. The first religions did not seem much concerned with ethics or inner life. Apparently it was fear that enthroned the first gods and entrenched the priesthoods—fear of invisible vengeful powers in the Earth, the skies, the waters. Religion began as worship of these forces through sacrifice and incantation. Gods hurled thunderbolts—until meteorology came. Stars ruled our destinies —until astronomy came. Witches and devils beset us—until medicine and psychology came.

But gradually religion also began to undergird morality and law. Thus religion changed—became vital and indispensable. The Church served in every civilized land as a comfort to the unhappy, the suffering, the bereaved—a comfort more precious than anything the machines brought.

Religion helped bring up children. It conferred meaning and dignity on the lowliest existence. It made for stable communities by transforming human convenants into solemn compacts with God. Until our day, every significant society has been held together with the help of religion.

The next big change that was to pass over human thinking began in the skies and first became visible little by little in the monasteries. Throughout the long darkness of medieval times, monks kept alight the learning of ancient Greek astronomers and studied "the conformation of the globe, the nature of the elements, the place of the stars," as Absalom of St. Victor wrote. Then in the thirteenth century the monk Roger Bacon, experimenting with pieces of glass that could magnify, prophesied the invention of the telescope and even more wondrous things. "In struments may be made by which the largest ships, with only one man guiding them, will be carried with incredible rapidity," he wrote. "A man, sitting at his ease and meditating, may beat the air with artificial wings."

His writings made a wide impression on learned minds of his time, particularly since his knowledge of astronomy had enabled him to prove that the Julian calendar was wrong in assuming a year was 365¼ days long. He demonstrated by astronomical means that each year was really only 365.2422 days, and concluded that in the slow turn of the centuries since Julius Caesar established this calendar the true spring equinox had crept up ten days ahead of the supposed equinox, so that Christians were celebrating Easter much later than they should. Eventually

Pope Gregory reformed the calendar and skipped ten days, thus catching up with the sun.

In 1543 a priest, Copernicus, published a book that jolted the Church to its foundations. He proved that God had not put man and the Earth at the center of the universe, as all God-fearing people believed. The Earth moved, he said, despite the evidence of men's senses. It whirled around the sun, and so did the other planets.

Martin Luther called Copernicus a fool. "Does this madman not know," he exclaimed, "that it was the sun and not the Earth that Joshua ordered to stand still?" Copernicus had cautiously withheld his book until the very end of his life, so the inquisition could not punish him for heresy in contradicting the Bible, but had to be content with placing his book on the Index Expurgatorius. Pope Paul III was inclined toward an open mind, for he knew that the Copernican theory explained the observed zigzags of the planets. Consequently a number of churchmen-scientists boldly taught that God's universe was not man-centered —whereupon one was burned and others were excommunicated.

But the great voyages of exploration, steering by the stars, had begun to open men's minds. Only the more dogmatic hierarchs saw any conflict with God in this liberation. Humble monks stood high on the roll of astronomers, inventors, and mechanics—for they were alert scholars and they saw different branches of learning cross-fertilizing each other, one science helping another. It was no accident that pioneer scientists of the seventeenth century, such as Galileo, Newton, Kepler, Descartes, Pascal, were all devout men. They believed in an orderly universe well-designed by God and waiting to be understood. They felt in touch with Him in each new glimpse of the laws of nature.

Their vision of God as the master mathematician and all-powerful engineer led us toward the machines. The structure of science seemed to them—and has seemed to many scientists since —preordained by hidden plans. As the noted scientist Vannevar Bush wrote in 1959:

It is almost as though it had once existed, and its building blocks had then been scattered and buried, each with its unique form so that it would fit only in its own peculiar position. . . . There are those men of rare vision, who can grasp well in advance just the block that is needed, who can tell by some subtle sense where it will be found, and who have uncanny skill in bringing it surely into the light. . . . There are also the old men, whose days of vigorous building are done, but who have lived long in the edifice, have learned to love it and have even grasped a suggestion of its ultimate meaning; and who sit in the shade and encourage the young men.

Kepler was so convinced he was deciphering one of God's blueprints, when he traced the clocklike movements of the celestial machinery, that he boasted in exaltation that the Author had waited six thousand years for His first reader. (The shocking news of Earth's true age was to come much later.) Similarly, seventeenth-century biologists viewed living creatures as marvelous intricate machines designed by an infinitely ingenious mechanic, and took them apart to discover how He built them. By analyzing them, man might himself become a counterfeiter of machines; might eventually build a seeing mechanism, a hearing mechanism, a flying mechanism, and so on.

By 1750 the groundwork was laid and the key inventions had been made. An army of experimenters, scientists, mechanics, was growing. They proclaimed the dawn and announced how marvelous the new day would be. But unconsciously they were also marking a shift in the seasons, and in fact a long cyclical change in the climate itself.

With the so-called Industrial Revolution of the eighteenth century, the machines came among all Western men. They proliferated. At the same time, for reasons half-hidden in Church histories of the past two centuries, theologians lost interest in science. They decided to concern themselves exclusively with souls; the flesh was unimportant, and the whole vast external world was only incidental. Perhaps it seldom occurred to them that God reveals Himself in the laboratory and the observatory as He does in the sanctuary, and that scientific discoveries are disclosures of God as significant as an exegesis of Holy Writ.

At any rate, most churchmen clung to beliefs that God answered prayers and worked unpredictable miracles, while scientists mostly scoffed at anything that could not be measured and charted. Probing the universe and its patterns, science found nowhere any certainty that the grand design had been drawn with man in mind. Man was a tiny, trivial, transient creature upon a mere speck of a galaxy in the great vault of intergalactic Space. In this galaxy alone there were more planets than men.

Still, whatever men could not understand or control, they entrusted to God. They founded this Republic, against terrifying odds, on the simple axiom from the Old Testament: "In God We Trust." For generations they spoke of "acts of God," even in legal contracts and insurance policies.

But now that science knows so much, now that nothing is left unpredictable beneath the visiting moon, what place is left for God? Shall religion be shut out from every field in which science makes firm pronouncements? Need we pray for healing when the pharmacy has wonder drugs? Does the good Samaritan lose his shirt? Why bother with the Golden Rule when we can skip town in case of scandal? Shall we whittle down God to merely "the God of the gaps," as some modern churchmen call Him?

There are no easy answers. It takes wisdom, not knowledge, for anyone to answer such questions for himself. Wisdom is not found in a computer or a telescope or a rocket test stand. Let us hope that posterity does not say of this generation, as Stephen Vincent Benét said of another, "They thought, because they had power, they had wisdom also."

It is in this perspective and against this background that we must look for the star within and try to determine whether we are truly angels as well as beasts. Can we, like our own silver ships hurtling through black nothingness, make internal adjustments that bring about a midcourse correction? In his book *The Human Predicament*, George W. Morgan gives us a fix on our position.

> The sheer weight of accumulated but uncontrolled knowledge and information, of print, views, discoveries, and interpretations, of methods and techniques, inflicts a paralyzing sense of impotence. The mind is overwhelmed. . . . The individual, feeling unable to gain a valid perspective of the world and of himself, is forced to regard both as innumerable isolated parts to be relinquished to a legion of experts.

To put it another way, science is now remote not only from the Church but from the mass of humanity. It talks incomprehensible jargon. The result is that the world has grown emptier for many people. Neither religion nor science speaks to them. There are no goals visible to them except material enrichment; nothing but emptiness to be filled with sex, drink, television, and travel. It is impossible to build a full life around an empty heart and an empty mind, as these people have vaguely sensed. Other people, feeling cut off, have lashed out angrily. Today they riot with the new Know-Nothings. The glory and poetry are gone.

So it seems clear that one adjustment needed in our midcourse correction is for us all to learn to talk with one another. Scientists and nonscientists, including churchmen, must stop talking to themselves and tune in on each other. They must try to understand and to make themselves understood. Beasts do not talk. Angels do. Men can.

This need to understand one another is coming to be widely recognized. Great centers of technical training, such as Cal Tech and MIT and the national military academies, have lately put in new courses in "the humanities" and made them requirements for graduation. They are tired of turning out merely hardheaded "practical" specialists who cannot explain their own specialties to outsiders and who cannot understand anyone else's interests.

Great corporations have begun recruiting generalists as well as technicians, liberal-arts graduates as well as engineers and accountants. Within their own organizations, as we saw in Chapter 11, they are breaking down the old-style human pyramids and moving toward fluid, flexible groups where discussion is easier. They are experimenting with such startling innovations as "sensitivity training" and "job enrichment" and "participative management." All of which means that they have suddenly seen themselves, and their people, as too machinelike.

The same ferment, in much more turbulent manifestations, is roiling campuses in many parts of the world. Sometimes with berserk fury that defeats their basic purpose, a whole generation is suddenly asserting that much teaching is pedantic and unenlightening; that students are entitled to an opinion of the curriculum and a voice in governing the processes of their own education. There has been violence on campuses before, but no such demands as these.

Many officials speak of recent insurrections in terms of doomsday. They say we have come to a time like the fall of Rome and the fall of the Bastille, when civilizations collapse because belief is dead. But others think that just the opposite is happening: passionate belief has come alive for the first time in centuries.

Laurence M. Gould, President Emeritus of Carleton College, is one of those who do not think the riots mean our civilization is defunct. "I think it will die when we no longer care," he says. "Arnold Toynbee has pointed out that 19 of 21 civilizations died from within and not by conquest. It happened slowly, in the quiet and the dark when no one was aware."

More and more people seem to be keenly aware that there is a lot wrong with us all. They notice a flatness in human life, a loss of depth as though a dimension had somehow dropped from the world. This was the same sort of awareness of something missing that brought the flowering of the Renaissance, as noted in Chapter 2, when the sparks from the monasteries set ablaze an Age of Exploration and discovery in the skies and on the seas.

Today's turmoil can be viewed as the pain and confusion that come when an age is dying and a new one is being born. They may well be, as some say, a revulsion (often incoherent) against bureaucratic indifference to man; against scientific unconcern about human consequences; against the compartmentalization and stratification of cities; against the regimentation of universities; against rat races and moneygrubbing and the organization man; against selfishness and wretchedness bred by dictatorships of all kinds.

But there is little humanism in blind confrontation and rejection. The human race is the only species, so far as we know, that can be humorous and compassionate and curious about others; can cherish beauty; can comprehend the past and visualize the future; can ask questions and try to explain. All of us sorely need to use these unique human attributes if the new age is to come to fruition.

"Dialogue" is a stale word in the vocabulary. And yet a candid exchange of ideas and a willingness to learn from one another are hard to generate. Many of us do not really want to talk about our differences. The process is unsettling and irritating and might force us to change. The safest thing is to look, act, and speak like everyone else in our own in-group or pressure group.

If our situation has changed too fast to suit us, maybe we need a new appraisal of our situation and our ideas. Maybe we must look around for some new ideas. Then too, our own ideas may be helpful to others, and we should take the necessary pains to explain them in language that others understand—and to revise them whenever they do not stand the test of free discussion.

Each element in life forms part of a cultural mesh—strengthening yet restraining one another, rippling across the mesh, all parts helping to shape the whole. In 1957 the mesh was broken. A fragment escaped and launched itself out on a separate path into Space.

The will to explore was loose again, after centuries in which it had found only tiny outlets. And suddenly man began to see the old vision of himself, faring forth boldly in search of new homes far away, instead of marching obediently to the measure of clocks and calendars and contracts. The Space Age has begun the newest, the ultimate quest of the human spirit. And all the elements of our cultural mesh have begun to feel its straining.

One of the phenomena of the breakdown of the Middle Ages was a turbulence that made men freebooters, pioneers, discoverers, rebels—breaking away from the tame old ways and the imprisonment of intellectual darkness. In the same way, the yeastiness of the Space Age may explain much of the worldwide human seething of the 1960's. What men do is shaped by how they see themselves: a vision of moving among the planets and extending the human species far outward instead of fighting among themselves. Before this supreme adventure of mankind can be completed, if ever, an eon may pass and Earth may grow cold and the human seed may be scattered among the stars.

But each step of this adventure will require higher ascension into a spiritual realm only half-familiar to us: the realm of cooperation. Our new vision implies a world where kindly feeling is common. The moon ship with its exquisite precision and mighty rocket engines is a stupendous feat of many minds; no Steinmetz or Edison or Da Vinci could have conceived it by himself. But now, having staged for the whole world this dramatic demonstration of superhuman skill and power, we will suffer a tragic letdown and anticlimax if we neglect to use our new-fledged attributes to improve the quality of life on Earth. The disappointment of expectant millions and the effluvia of rampant machines will breed poisons almost sure to destroy our social system.

We know now that we can do anything that needs to be done. It is simply a matter of finding the right combinations of human talents and Earthly resources, of making the right social arrangements. This will take ever-increasing *exploration* by each of us, and ever-increasing *communication* between all of us.

But this is the way to fulfillment. If we try to make ourselves content with the happiness of the pig, our suppressed potentialities will make us miserable. Whenever man turns an especially sharp corner in history, he feels uncertain. No wonder so many people feel uncertain as we plunge into the Space Age! Yet at this same time most of us feel—when we stop and listen to our innermost hearts—a great new hope, an intuitive hunch that God's purpose is at work in us as we go forth. So let us face this dawning future, participate actively instead of just letting it happen, and help to plan it as trustees for the generations yet unborn.

Compared to the wondrous years ahead, all our recorded history with its magnificent processions of saints, seers, poets, philosophers, law-givers, and light-givers, all the mighty dead and the billions of humble dead—all these will seem only a prologue to a drama beyond even the dreams of mankind's ancient gods.